CONSTABLE'S RUSSIAN LIBRARY, under the Editorship of STEPHEN GRAHAM

WAR AND CHRISTIANITY

UNIFORM WITH THIS VOLUME

THE SWEET-SCENTED NAME
By FEDOR SOLOGUB
With an Introduction
By STEPHEN GRAHAM

Ex. Crown 8vo.   4s. 6d. net.

"It seems to me to be the greatest literary treasure of its kind that has appeared during the present year."—*The Daily News.*

"Sologub is one of the most widely read of contemporary Russian authors."—*The Athenæum.*

LONDON
CONSTABLE & CO. LIMITED

War and Christianity:

From the Russian Point of View
Three Conversations by

Vladimir Solovyof

With an Introduction by

Stephen Graham

London
Constable & Company Ltd

First Published July, 1915.

Reprinted October, 1915.

Printed in Great Britain.

PREFACE

VLADIMIR SOLOVYOF, the author of this book, is Russia's greatest philosopher and one of the greatest of her poets, a serene and happy writer. He was born in 1853 and died in 1901, that is, he flourished in Russia during the same years that Nietzsche lived in Germany. He was a seeker and also a seer, a thinker and also a singer. His life is not marked by irritability, and it did not culminate in mental and psychic collapse as did the life of Nietzsche. Probably life was easier for a man of genius in Russia than in Germany—there are wider spaces there, more freedom, more tenderness between man and man, less materialism, less selfishness, less to send one mad.

Solovyof came from a happy home and of a literary family. His father, Serge Mikhalovitch Solovyof, was a historian; his mother, a Little Russian of old family and culture, was proud to remind her children of a kinsman who had been a great philosopher in his day. At home there was an atmosphere of real things—never any of the cheap wit and vulgarism and mental meanness that so often sterilise the creative intelligence of otherwise wonderful children. There was much reading aloud and many lively discussions about life and religion. Every one of Solovyof's brothers and sisters achieved distinction in life and letters later on. Vladimir was, however, the greatest and showed his gifts from the first.

The young man's distinctive tone in thought was opposition to positivism, humanitarianism and the ideas of Western civilisation, and throughout his student days he propounded in many arguments a lively belief in Russia and the Russian idea, in orthodoxy and mysticism. But with all his brilliance he was also an industrious scholar. He graduated in 1873, and gave many of the succeeding years of youth to research and study. He held a professorship for a short while, but gave up his chair in 1882, and the remaining eighteen years of his life were devoted almost entirely to literary work.

As a poet he was, nearest to Féte, one of the most delicate of Russian poets. Solovyof was the first poet philosopher of his country, the first to speak simply and beautifully in verse of the most difficult problems of man's life and religion. In his works you may seek and find the Russian idea, the Eastern Christian point of view. His philosophy derives in part from gnostic Christianity, and is associated with the idea of St. Sophia rather than the idea of St. Peter, with eternal wisdom rather than eternal law.

It would be impossible to sum up in a sentence the author's majestical vision of life, but we may cite an exclamation from one of his poems :

"All evil is powerless, man is for ever, and God is with us!"

PREFACE

In national culture Solovyof owned Dostoieffsky as his prophet. With Dostoieffsky he was one of the great spiritual leaders of the Russian people. He was in all his work and faith opposed to Tolstoy, considering Tolstoyism to be a sort of moral atrophy. Yet he never attacked Tolstoy by name, and was never mixed up in any acrid controversy. The accompanying volume is one of the chief of those in which Tolstoyism and positivism are combated. At the present moment, when recurring war has caused much heart-searching in the minds of Christian people, it has been thought most fitting to issue a translation of this Russian book.

War has not prompted so many misgivings in Christian Russia as it has done in the humanitarian and materialistic West. It is felt that—

"Religion is never shaken down by war, but logicians are shaken in their logic, agnosticism is shaken, materialism is shaken, atheism is shaken, positivism is shaken. The intellectual dominance is shaken and falls, the spiritual powers are allowed to take possession of men's being."

Solovyof issued "War and Christianity" on Easter Day, 1900, the year before his death. According to Valery Brusof, one of the most interesting of contemporary Russian essayists—

"Towards the end of Solovyof's life a sort of special power and intensity of perception seemed to show itself in his work. The poet and thinker approached the most sacred problems of contemporary man. . . . Everyone was listening to the powerful voice of Solovyof as to the words of a master; his right to judge was acknowledged. . . . Death unexpectedly cut short this teaching so necessary to us. . . . But, bewaring of superfluous lamentation, let us call to mind that he himself tried to find a sense and a moral indispensability even in the shot of Dantes and the destruction of the 'godly phial' as if it were a potter's vessel."

Especial thanks are due to Mr. Edward Cazalet, of the Anglo-Russian Literary Society, who translated Conversation II., and to Mr. W. J. Barnes and Mr. H. H. Haynes, who translated Conversation III., and to Mr. Barnes, who saw through the proofs.

STEPHEN GRAHAM.

LONDON,
April, 1915.

THE SCENE

In the garden of one of those villas which, at the foot of the Alps, look down on the blue depths of the Mediterranean, there met one summer five Russians: an old general, of many campaigns, we shall call him the General; a politician, a "father of the Senate," resting from the theoretical and practical occupations of State affairs, we shall call him the Politician; a young prince, a moralist and popular teacher, responsible for the editing of various more or less helpful pamphlets on moral and social questions, we shall call him the Prince; a lady of middle age, interested in all that concerns human beings, she is the Lady; and the fifth was a gentleman of doubtful age and social position, let us call him Mr. Z.

I was a silent listener to all their conversations, some of which appeared to me to have much interest, and whilst they were fresh in my memory I wrote them down. The first conversation was begun in my absence. I believe it started *apropos* of some newspaper article or peace pamphlet on the subject of the campaign against war and military service, which was being carried on by the Baroness Luttner and Mr. Stead, following in the footsteps of Tolstoy.

The Politician, on being asked by the Lady

whether he thought the peace movement was a good one, gave it as his opinion that it was well-intentioned and useful. At that, the General got angry and began to make satirical jests at the expense of these three writers, calling them the true pillars of State wisdom, guiding constellations on the political horizon, even calling them the three whales of Russia. The Politician remarked that there were other *fish*. This remark caused Mr. Z. to collapse with laughter, and he forced both the speakers to confess that they considered a whale was a fish, and even persuaded them to give a conjoint definition of what they thought a fish to be, that is, an animal belonging partly to the marine department and partly to the department of marine communications. I think, however, this was an invention of Mr. Z. Be that as it may, I was not fortunate enough to obtain the real beginning of the conversation. Being afraid to compose out of my own head after the model of Plato and his imitators, I began my transcript with the words of the General which I heard as I approached the speakers.

WAR AND CHRISTIANITY

FIRST CONVERSATION

" Audiatur et prima pars."

GENERAL (*agitated, stands up and then sits down again, speaking in rapid gestures*).—No, permit me! Tell me only one thing: does a " Christ-serving and worthy Russian militancy " [1] exist or not? Yes or no?

POLITICIAN (*stretching himself on his deck-chair and speaking in a tone which reminds one of something between that of the careless gods of Epicurus, of a Prussian officer and of Voltaire*).—Does a Russian army exist? Obviously it exists. Surely you haven't heard that it is dismissed?

GENERAL.—Now, don't sham. You understand quite well about what I am speaking. I ask, have I still the right as before to consider the existent army as a worthy Christ-loving militancy—or is this designation out of date and should we change it for another?

POLITICIAN.—Eh ... so that's what you're worrying yourself about? You shouldn't address that question to me, but rather to the department of heraldry where the various titles are supervised.

[1] A traditional title of the Russian army.

Mr. Z.—The department of heraldry would probably answer that the use of old titles is not objected to legally. Did not the last Prince Luzinian call himself King of Cyprus, and nobody said him nay, though not only did he not rule Cyprus, but was not even rich enough to drink Cyprus wine? So why shouldn't our contemporary army have the title of a Christ-serving militancy?

General.—What has title got to do with it? Is white or black a title? Is sweet or bitter a title? Hero or scoundrel—are they titles?

Mr. Z.—Yes, of course. I wasn't giving my own point of view, but rather the legality of the matter.

Lady (*to Politician*).—Why are you hedging over words? You may be sure the General wished to put a real question with his " Christ-serving militancy."

General.—Thank you. I did wish, and do still wish, to say just this : For centuries, and up to yesterday itself, every military man had a clear conscience, whether it were common soldier or field-marshal it was all the same ; he knew and felt that he was serving a good and important end. He knew it was not something merely useful, as for instance, sanitation, or laundry-work, but in the highest sense, something fine, noble, honourable, something in which in the past the very best people had served, the first people, the leaders of nations, heroes. Our work has always been consecrated and magnified in the churches and has become famous by general consent. But suddenly one fine morning we are told that we have got to forget all that, and that we ought to interpret our position in this God's world entirely in the opposite sense. We have to recognise that the profession of which we were so proud is something evil and damaging, contrary to God's commandments and human intelligence, the most dreadful trouble and calamity. We are told that all nations must combine to stop it, and that its complete abolition is really only a matter of time.

PRINCE.—But surely, you must have heard some time or other, earlier in your career, voices which condemned war and military service as a survival of ancient cannibalism?

GENERAL.—How not hear it? I heard it and read it in various languages, but I cannot say it made much impression on me. I heard it and forgot it. But now we've come to a different position. There's no getting past it. So I ask: How do we stand? How ought I, that is, how ought any army man to consider himself, how ought he to look upon himself—as a real man or as an unnatural monster? Ought I to take myself seriously as a worker in an honest and important cause, or should I be horror-stricken by it, repent of it, and humbly beg each civilian to forgive me my professional accursedness?

POLITICIAN.—Why put the question so fantastically? It is as if we'd been asking you to do something special. The new demands of society are not made upon you, but upon diplomatists and other civil people in authority who are very little interested either in your accursedness or in your "service of Christ." We only ask one thing of you, now as before, to fulfil without asking questions the orders of your superiors.

GENERAL.—As you are not interested in military matters you naturally think I put the matter fantastically. You evidently don't seem to know that on certain occasions the commands of the authorities are to the effect that we act without asking for commands.

POLITICIAN.—For instance?

GENERAL.—For instance: imagine that I am appointed by authority as head of a complete military circuit. I should have all manner of duties in that position, managing the troops entrusted to me. I should have to train and confirm in them a certain way of thinking. I should have to train their wills in a certain direction and tune their feelings to a certain harmony. In a word, I should have to bring them up to their destiny. Very well. I should have to give general commands to the troops for the attainment of that end, under my name and personal responsibility. Well, if I addressed myself to superior authority to find out exactly what I should do, should I not be put down at once by them as an old fool, the first time I did it, and have to go into retirement at the second? That means, I am simply obliged to act on my own responsibility and interpret the spirit of war and the will of the authorities as best I can—since to ask about it would be either stupidity or audacity. But I am asking this question now about our position because the *spirit* which has been one and the same from Sargon and Assurbanipal to William the Second appears suddenly to be in doubt. Until yesterday I knew that I had to train and confirm in our troops nothing other than just this military spirit—the readiness of each soldier to kill his enemies and to be, if necessary, killed—and for that it is absolutely necessary to be perfectly sure that war is something holy. Suddenly the habitual confidence of the officer loses its foundation and military deeds are deprived of their "moral-religious sanction," to use a learned phrase.

POLITICIAN.—That's all fearfully exaggerated. There has been no radical change in the accepted point of view. Even formerly, everyone always knew that war was evil and the less of it the better, and, on the other hand, wise people know now that it is a kind of evil which cannot yet be removed once and for all in our time. The problem is not the complete abolition of war, but its gradual limitation and isolation within certain narrow boundaries. The fundamental notion about war remains what it has always been, *i.e.*, that it is an inevitable evil, a calamity which must be endured upon extreme occasions.

GENERAL.—And only that?

POLITICIAN.—Yes, that only.

GENERAL (*jumping from his seat*).—Did you ever by any chance look in the Saints?

POLITICIAN.—You mean in the Calendar? I've had to look up names of patron saints, the name-days of my friends and relatives.

GENERAL.—And have you remarked the sorts of saints in the Calendar?

POLITICIAN. —There were various sorts.
GENERAL.—But of what calling?
POLITICIAN.—And of various callings, I fancy.
GENERAL.—Well, that's just it. They are not so very various.
POLITICIAN.—What do you mean? You don't mean to say that they're all military men?
GENERAL. —Not all; but half are.
POLITICIAN. —Oh, again, what exaggeration!
GENERAL. —Well, we can't go over them one by one. But I affirm that the saints of our own Russian Church belong to two classes only: they are either monks of various grades, or princes. And to be a prince meant in old time to be a warrior. We have no other saints—of course, I am speaking of men-saints, they are all either monks or soldiers.
LADY.—But you've forgotten our fanatics, General!
GENERAL.—I haven't forgotten them at all, but they were a sort of irregular monks. What the Cossacks are to the army, they were for monasticism. What's more, if you can find for me among the Russian saints one white priest, or a merchant, or a deacon, or a chancellor's clerk, or a citizen, or a peasant, or, in one word, any representative of any profession other than that of monk or soldier—you can have all I shall bring back from Monte Carlo next Sunday.
POLITICIAN.—Thank you. You can keep your treasure and your half of the saints. But tell me, please, what did you want to deduce from this discovery or observation of yours? Surely you don't

WAR AND CHRISTIANITY

mean to argue that only monks and soldiers can be moral patterns?

GENERAL.—You haven't altogether guessed my meaning. I have known many virtuous people amongst the white clergy, amongst bankers, amongst officials, and amongst peasants. The most virtuous being I can call to mind is the peasant nurse-girl of one of my friends. But we are not speaking of that. My point really is—how could so many soldiers have found place side by side with monks and have been given a preference to ordinary civilians if their profession was a tolerated evil, such as, for instance, the liquor business or something even worse? It is clear that the Christian nations who showed their thoughts by the recognition of sainthood not only respected, but even specially respected the military calling, and that of all worldly professions they reckoned the military alone to be the best training place for sanctity. And that point of view is not compatible with the present movement to abolish war.

POLITICIAN.—Oh, have I said that there has been *no* change? Undoubtedly there has been some desirable change in point of view. The religious aureole which once surrounded war and warriors in the eyes of the crowd has now been taken away. That's so. But we had got to that point long since. And whom does that practically affect? The clergy perhaps, since the preparation of aureoles belongs to its department. But the clergy have got a good deal still to get rid of. What they cannot preserve literally they interpret in an allegorical sense, and, for the rest, take refuge in blessed silence and blessed forgetfulness.

PRINCE.—Yes, the blessed adaptation to new ideas has commenced. I follow our religious literature pretty closely for my own publications. And I have already had the pleasure of reading in two journals that Christianity unconditionally condemns war.

GENERAL.—Surely not.

PRINCE.—Yes, I couldn't believe my eyes. But I can show it you.

POLITICIAN (*to General*).—You see! But why should that worry you. You are people of deeds, not of fine words. Professional *amour-propre* and vanity, eh? That's not a good state of things. But all the same, I repeat, that in practice all remains as before. Though the system of militarism which has prevented us breathing these last thirty years must now disappear, yet troops in certain dimensions will remain—as many as are considered indispensable. And from them will be demanded the same military qualities as before.

GENERAL.—Oh, now you're asking milk from a dead cow. Who will provide you with the military qualities when the primal inspiration of these military qualities has been removed—the faith in the holiness of the work? And this faith cannot remain, once it is held that war is an evil and a calamity only tolerated on extreme occasions.

POLITICIAN.—Oh, we shan't ask military men to hold that opinion. Let them consider themselves the first people in the world—whose business is it? Didn't I say that Prince Luzinian was permitted to call himself King of Cyprus as long as he didn't ask us to provide him with money to buy Cyprus wine? Don't tempt yourselves to our pockets more than you need, that's all. And then, if you will, you may remain in your own eyes the salt of the earth and the flower of mankind; who is to prevent you?

GENERAL.—He says in our own eyes! Are we talking on the moon? Are we going to keep our military forces in a Torricellian vacuum to save them from outside influences? This in the time of universal military service, with conscripts who have only to serve short terms, in the time of cheap newspapers? No, the matter is clear enough. Once military service became obligatory for all and each, and at the same time this negative attitude towards military work became recognised throughout society, beginning with the representatives of the State, as you for instance, then undoubtedly that negative attitude must be assimilated by the officers and the soldiers themselves. If people came to look on military service as merely an inevitable evil, then no one would voluntarily choose the military profession as a life career, unless indeed it were some sport of Nature who could find no other refuge; and all those who against their will are obliged to bear arms for a while will bear them in the same spirit as penal convicts bear their chains. In the face of that, what have you to say about the relation of military qualities to the military spirit?

MR. Z.—I have always been convinced that, after the bringing in of universal military service, the final dismissal of the troops and the break-up of separate States is only a question of time, and a time not very far distant, considering the present tempo of history.

GENERAL.—Perhaps you're right.

PRINCE.—I will even affirm that you are certainly right, though it never came into my head till this moment. But that's splendid. Only think of it: militarism brings forth as its extreme expression the system of universal military service, and, thanks just to that, there perish not only the most modern form of militarism, but all the ancient foundations of the military idea. Wonderful!

LADY.—The Prince's face has become quite gay. That is good. He had been going about with such a gloomy expression—not at all that which becomes a " true Christian."

PRINCE.—Yes, we are surrounded already by too many sad things; one joy remains mine, however— the knowledge of the inevitable triumph of reason over all things.

MR. Z.—There isn't the slightest doubt that militarism in Europe and in Russia will eat itself up and die of surfeit, but what sort of joys and triumphs will result from that fact remains to be seen.

PRINCE.—How? Do you mean to say you have any doubt but that war and the military business is anything but an unconditional and extreme evil from which humanity has got to free itself absolutely, and as soon as it can? Do you mean to say you doubt that a complete and rapid disappearance of this cannibalism would not be, under any circumstances, a triumph of reason and goodness?

Mr. Z.—I am absolutely convinced to the contrary.

Prince.—That is to say?

Mr. Z.—. . . that war is not an unconditional evil, and that peace is not an unconditional good, or, speaking more simply, it is possible to have a *good war;* it is also possible to have a *bad peace.*

Prince.—Oh, now I see the difference between your point of view and that of the General. He thinks that war is always good and peace is always bad.

General.—No, no. I understand perfectly that war can be upon occasion a very bad affair, for instance, when we are beaten, as at Narva or Austerlitz; and peace can be splendid, as for instance, the peace of Nishstadt or Kutchuk-Kainardzh.

Lady.—That seems to be another variation of the famous remark of some Kaffir or Hottentot, who told the missionary that he understood the difference between good and evil quite well: good was when he carried off other people's wives and cattle, evil was when others carried off his.

General.—The African let that fall accidentally, I made that humorous remark on purpose. But now I'd like to hear how clever people determine the moral point of view about war.

Politician.—Ah, if our "clever people" would only put aside scholasticism and metaphysics when they come to such a clear, historically conditioned problem.

Prince.—Clear—from what point of view?

POLITICIAN.—My point of view is the ordinary European one, which, by the way, nowadays, even in other parts of the world, educated people are beginning to assimilate.

PRINCE.—And its essence is, of course, that everything is comparative, and that an unconditional difference between *ought* and *ought not*, between good and bad, must never be allowed. Isn't that it?

MR. Z.—Beg pardon; this point of dispute is surely futile. I, for instance, whole-heartedly acknowledge an irreconcilable opposition between moral good and evil, but, even holding that opinion, it is still quite clear to me that war and peace cannot be checked off in that way, and that it would be impossible to say that war was all black and peace was all white.

PRINCE.—But you are making a contradiction in terms. If something which is in itself evil, as for instance, murder, can under certain circumstances be good, when, for instance, you choose to call it war, then where will you put your unconditional distinction between good and evil?

MR. Z.—How simple it is for you. Every murder is an unconditional evil, war is murder; therefore war is an unconditional evil. A syllogism of the first order. But you have forgotten that both the larger and the smaller premisses have yet to be demonstrated, so consequently your conclusion still hangs in the air.

POLITICIAN.—Didn't I say that we should drop into scholasticism?

LADY.—Yes. What *are* they talking about?

POLITICIAN.—About the larger and the smaller premiss.

MR. Z.—Forgive me. We shall get to business in a moment. So you affirm that on any occasion to take away another person's life is unconditional evil?

PRINCE.—Without doubt.

MR. Z.—And to be killed—is that an unconditional evil, or not?

PRINCE. — According to the Hottentots, the answer is yes, but we were speaking about moral evil, and that can consist only in the personal actions of a reasoning being, it cannot consist in what happens to a being against his will. That means, to be killed—just as to die from cholera or influenza—not only is not an unconditional evil, but even is not evil. Socrates and the Stoics taught us that in their day.

MR. Z.—Well, for people of such antiquity I will not take it upon myself to answer. But your idea of unconditional evil goes a bit lame when we take into consideration the moral significance of a murder. According to you it works out that an unconditional evil consists in causing to another something which in itself is not even evil. As you will, but the theory limps a little there. However, we will dismiss this question of limping, lest through it we should really climb into an academic discussion. The point is that the evil of murder consists not in the physical fact of the deprivation of life, but in the moral reason of that fact, that is, in the evil will of the murderer. You agree?

PRINCE.—Of course. Without that evil will there

is no murder. There is only misfortune or carelessness.

Mr. Z.—It is quite clear when the will to kill is completely absent, as for instance in the case of an unsuccessful surgical operation. But it is possible to imagine a different situation, when the will, although it has not the direct aim of taking away the life of a man, has yet agreed to that idea as possible upon an extreme occasion. Would a murder resulting from such a state of will be, from your point of view, unconditionally evil?

Prince.—Yes, of course, once the will agrees to murder.

Mr. Z.—But surely it happens that a will, though agreeing to the idea of murder, is still not an evil will, and that consequently, murder cannot be an unconditional evil, even from the subjective side.

Prince.—That's quite incomprehensible. . . . However, I guess what you're after. You mean the famous instance when in a wild district a father is face to face with an engaged scoundrel who is about to fling himself on his innocent (for greater effect add the word little) daughter, and the father being unable to protect her otherwise, slays the would-be ravisher. I've heard the argument a thousand times.

Mr. Z.—The remarkable thing, however, is not that you have heard it a thousand times, but that no one has ever heard from those who think like you even a fair-seeming objection to the argument.

Prince.—But what is there to answer?

Mr. Z.—There, there. Well, if you do not wish to answer in the form of an objection, then state a direct and positive case to the effect that on all occasions without exception, and consequently in this of which we are speaking, to abstain from material opposition of evil is better than to employ force with the risk of killing an evil and dangerous man.

PRINCE.—What sort of generalisation can there be for a unique case? Once you have agreed that murder in general is in the moral sense evil, then it is clear that in every single instance it will be evil also.

LADY.—Oh, but that's weak.

MR. Z.—It is even very weak, Prince. That it is generally better not to kill than to kill, we are all agreed, and there is no argument about it. The question is about separate occasions. It is asked: Is the general or generally accepted rule not to kill really an absolute rule permitting no exceptions whatever, neither upon a unique occasion nor under any circumstances whatsoever, or does it permit, be it even one exception, and become therefore a rule which is not absolute, not unconditional?

PRINCE.—No, I don't agree to such a formal statement of the question. To what end? If I admit that in your exceptional example specially thought out for argument . . .

LADY (*reproachfully*).—Dear, dear!

GENERAL (*ironically*).—Oh-ho-ho!

PRINCE (*paying no attention*).—Granting that in your specially-thought-out instance to kill is better than not to kill—as a matter of fact I, of course, do not admit such a thing, but supposing you are right, supposing also that your instance is not one specially thought out for argument but is something which is real, though, as you would agree, most rare and exceptional. We are talking of war, are we not? A general and universal phenomenon. And you will not dare to affirm that Napoleon or Moltke or Skobelef were to be found in any position in the remotest degree resembling that of a father obliged to protect his daughter from a savage.

LADY.—Ah, that's better. Bravo, mon Prince!

MR. Z.—Certainly. A clever extrication from an unpleasant question. But allow me, however, to state the logical and historical link between the two phenomena, murder and war. For that purpose let us take up our example without, however, those particulars which seem to strengthen it, but which, as a matter of fact, really weaken its significance. The fact that he who murdered was a father and she whom he protected was his daughter is not necessary to us, in that the question loses its ethical significance in the domain of natural moral feelings: parental love would, of course, force the father to strike the evil-doer without waiting to decide the question had he or had he not the right to do it from the highest moral standpoint. So let us abandon the father and take a childless moralist before whose eyes some weak fellow-creature, altogether unknown to him, is suddenly subjected to the furious assault of a wild miscreant. According to you, this moralist should fold his arms and preach virtue whilst the monster is tearing his victim; is that not it? According to you, this moralist would not feel in himself any moral impulse to stop the monster by material force with the possibility and even probability of killing. And if the crime is committed to the accompaniment of his fine words, do you mean to say that his conscience will not reproach him, and that he will not be ashamed of himself and disgusted with himself?

PRINCE.—It is possible that a moralist who did not believe in the reality of moral order, or who forgot that God was not in violence but in truth, might feel so.

LADY.—Ah, that's very well said. Now you answer something.

MR. Z.—I answer that I should have liked it to be said still better, more directly and more simply. I suppose you wished to say that a moralist who actually believed in God's truth should have turned to God with prayer that the evil deed be not committed, or asking for a moral miracle, the sudden turning of the evil-doer to the way of truth, or asking for a material miracle, the sudden paralysis of the man . . .

LADY.—It could be done without paralysis. The murderer might take fright at something or be in some other way diverted from his evil intention.

MR. Z.—That's all the same, because the miracle is not in the actual happening, but in the expediency of the happening, be it in physical paralysis or in some sort of mental agitation. In any case, the Prince's means of preventing evil-doing lies either in prayer or in miracle.

PRINCE.—What do you mean? Why prayer, why miracle?

Mr. Z.—If not, what then?

Prince.—Once I believe that the world is governed on good and reasonable principles I believe nothing that is contrary to the will of God can happen.

Mr. Z.—Beg pardon! How old are you?

Prince.—What do you mean by that question?

Mr. Z.—Nothing offensive, I assure you. Thirty?

Prince.—Over thirty.

Mr. Z.—Then you certainly must have seen, or, if you have not seen, must have heard, or, if you have not heard, must have read in the newspapers, that evil and immoral deeds do, however, take place upon this world.

Prince.—Well?

Mr. Z.—Well, that means that moral order or truth or the will of God is not absolutely realised upon the world . . .

Politician.—At last to business. If evil exists, then the gods either cannot or do not wish to prevent it. Gods in the sense of all-powerful or blessed forces do not exist. Old, but true.

Lady.—Oh, you!

General.—We have talked ourselves to that point. Philosophise and your head goes round.

Prince.—But that's bad philosophy! As if God's will were connected with our vague conceptions of good and evil.

Mr. Z.—With certain vague conceptions it is not connected, but with the true understanding of good it is connected in the closest way. Otherwise, if good and evil are indifferent to the Godhead, you have refuted your own argument, Prince.

PRINCE.—How is that?

MR. Z.—Because if it's all the same for the Godhead whether a savage under the influence of brutal passion destroys a weak and delicate being, then long since the Godhead must have found nothing objectionable in the man who, under the influence of compassion, destroys the savage. You will certainly not set yourself to defend anything so absurd as that the murder of a weak and innocent being is not evil before God, but that the murder of a strong and evil one is.

PRINCE.—That seems to you absurd because you lay the emphasis in the wrong place. What is morally important is not who is killed, but who kills. You yourself called the evil-doer a savage, that is, a being without conscience or reason; and how could there be moral evil, therefore, in his actions?

LADY.—Oh, oh! What question is there of a savage in the literal sense? It's all the same as if I said to my daughter, "What stupidities you are saying, my angel!" and you began to take me to task and say "Can angels say stupidities?" What a poor argument this is!

PRINCE.—Excuse me. I know, of course, that the savage is also a man, but all the same, it is not possible that a man with reason and conscience should commit such a crime.

MR. Z.—Of course a man acting like a beast loses reason and conscience in the sense that he ceases to listen to their voice, but that the man is without reason or conscience altogether remains to be shown, and meanwhile I shall continue of opinion that the brutal man is distinguished from us, not by the absence of reason and conscience, but only by his own determination to act contrary to them at the enticement of the beast in himself, but the beast is in us also, only we commonly keep him in durance. The man of whom we are speaking had loosed the beast from his fetters; but fetters were there though not being used. In general, that's it, and if the Prince doesn't agree with you quickly, hoist him with his own petard. If the evil-doer were only a beast, one absolutely without reason or conscience, then to kill him would be all the same as to kill a wolf or a tiger who had been attacking a man—even the society for the protection of animals does not forbid that.

PRINCE.—But you again forget that whatever the state of that man's mind, whether reason and conscience were in complete atrophy or whether he acted with conscious immorality, the question is not about him, but about you yourselves: your reason and conscience are not atrophied, and therefore you would not consciously disregard what they demand of you—you would not have killed that man, whatever sort of man he were.

MR. Z.—Of course I shouldn't have killed him if reason and conscience had unconditionally forbidden it. But put it to yourself that my reason and conscience advise me to act another way, and that way seems to me more reasonable and conscientious.

PRINCE.—Let us hear an example. It would be curious.

MR. Z.—And first of all let us admit that reason and conscience can count at least to three . . .

GENERAL.—Oh-ho ; oh-ho !

MR. Z.—And therefore reason and conscience, since they do not wish to give false verdicts, will not say to me two, when the answer is three.

GENERAL (*impatiently*).—Ts-s !

PRINCE.—This is all beyond me !

MR. Z.—Well, according to you, reason and conscience tell me only about myself and about the evil-doer, but the whole matter, according to you, is in that I do not lay a finger upon him. But we must not forget the third person, and he appears to me to be the most important, the victim of the outrage, the man demanding my support. You always forget about him, but conscience speaks of him, and speaks, I think, first of all. The will of God is that I save this victim, according to possibility, sparing the evil-doer, but in any case, I must give the help which is in my power ; admonition if that will do, if not, then material force, and only in the event of my arms being tied need I turn to the last means, seeking aid from above by prayer, that is, by the highest exercise of good-will, whence as a matter of fact I am convinced a miracle would derive when necessary. But which of these means of giving help to the victim it is necessary to employ depends on the spiritual and phenomenal conditions of the event. There is only one unconditional thing

here, and that is, that I help him who is suffering;
that is what my conscience says.

GENERAL.—Hurrah! The centre is broken.

PRINCE.—I do not look so widely. My conscience
in such a case is more definite, and expresses itself
more shortly: Thou shalt not kill—that is the
whole answer. Moreover, I do not see that we have
yet advanced an iota in this argument. If I again
agreed with you, that in the position which you
imagine, any man, even one morally developed and
deeply conscientious, could under the influence of
sympathy, not having time to obtain mentally a
clear notion of the moral quality of his act, commit
a murder, what follows with regard to the fundamental issue? Are we to suppose that Tamerlane
or Alexander of Macedon or Lord Kitchener killed
or forced others to kill for the protection of weak
and delicate beings who were in danger of assault at
the hand of evil-doers?

MR. Z.—This juxtaposition of Tamerlane and
Alexander of Macedon promises poorly for our historical sense, but since you, for the second time, turn
impatiently to this general domain of activity, then
permit me to quote an historical event which may
help us to connect the question of personal protection
with the question of governmental protection. It
was in the twelfth century at Kiev. The appanaged
princes were even then apparently of your opinion
with regard to war, and holding that quarrelling
and fighting should be confined to home, they would
not agree to go out to fight the Poloftsi, saying that
they would be sorry to cause people the calamity

WAR AND CHRISTIANITY

of war. To that the Grand Duke Vladimir Monomakh made the following reply: "You are sorry for these rascals, but you forget that Spring is coming. . . . The peasant will go out with his horse to plough. The Poloftsi will come, kill the peasant, and lead off his horse; they will come in great numbers, massacre all the peasants, carry off all the women and children, drive off the cattle and burn the village. Aren't you sorry for these people? I am sorry for them, and for that reason call you against the Poloftsi." On that occasion the princes were put to shame, and the land had protection under the rule of Vladimir. But they afterwards returned to their peace-loving state, avoided exterior wars, and quarrelled at home and made scandals, and it ended for Russia with the advance of the Mongol hordes, and for the actual descendants of these princes, it ended with the kind of entertainment which history brought them in the shape of Ivan IV.

PRINCE.—This is all beyond me. You cite an event which never occurred to any of us, and certainly never will occur, and call up some Vladimir Monomakh, who perhaps never existed at all, and with whom, in any case, we have nothing whatever to do . . .

LADY.—*Parlez pour vous, monsieur*.

MR. Z.—Why, you, Prince, are one of those who came to us with Rurik.

PRINCE.—They say so, but what interest to me, do you think, are Rurik, Sinius, and Truvor?

LADY.—I think that not to know about one's own forefathers is to be like children who think they were found in a kitchen garden and beneath a cabbage.

PRINCE.—And what about those unfortunates who don't happen to have any forefathers?

MR. Z.—Every one has at his disposal very circumstantial and instructive memoirs left him by his forefathers—I mean, national and universal history.

PRINCE.—But these memoirs cannot determine for us the question what are we to be *now*, what ought we to do *now*. Admit that Vladimir Monomakh did exist, and was not simply the imagination of some monk; admit even that he was an excellent man and was sincerely sorry for the peasants, in any case he was right to fight with the Poloftsi, because in those wild times moral conscience had not triumphed over the coarse Byzantine understanding of Christianity, and it did permit people to kill those whom they deemed evil-doers; but how can we act so, once that we have understood that murder is an evil, something contrary to the will of God, forbidden from of old by God's commandment, when we know that it cannot be permitted us under any guise, under any name, and cannot cease to be evil when instead of being the killing of one it becomes the killing of thousands under the name of war? It is first of all a question of personal conscience.

GENERAL.—Well, if it is a matter of personal conscience, permit me to make the following personal report. I am a man who in the moral sense, as of course in most other senses, am altogether mediocre —neither black nor white, but grey. I have not evinced either special virtue or special sin. But in all good acts there is always a difficulty in weighing their merit; you can never be sure whether your conscience had been obeyed, whether your conscience stands for real good or only for a kind of mental softness, a habit of life, or an impulse of vanity. Good acts always seem to be in a small way. In the whole of my life I only remember one good occasion which it would be impossible to name small, but I know absolutely that then there was no doubt whatever about my impulse; I acted solely at the dictates of a good power. It was the one occasion in life when I experienced a complete moral satisfaction, where I fell even into a sort of ecstasy because I had acted without reflection or hesitation. My act remains till now, and will of course remain for ever, my purest memory. Well, and that one good act of mine was a murder, and not by any means a small murder, for in a quarter of an hour I killed considerably more than a thousand men.

LADY.—*Quelles blagues!* And I thought that you were—serious.

GENERAL.—Altogether serious; I could bring witnesses. Certainly I did not kill with my hands, with these sinful hands, but with the aid of six pure, sinless, steel cannon, with the most virtuous and beneficial shrapnel.

LADY.—What good was there in that?

GENERAL.—Well, of course, although I am a military man, and, even according to our present style, a militarist, I should not call the simple destruction of a few thousands of ordinary people something good, be they Germans or Hungarians or Englishmen or Turks. This was something quite special. I cannot even now speak about it with equanimity. It stirred up my soul so much.

LADY.—Well, tell us it quickly.

GENERAL.—Since I mentioned the cannon, you no doubt guess that it was in the last Turkish war. I was in the Third Caucasian Army. After the third of October . . .

LADY.—What third of October?

GENERAL.—That was when the fight on the heights of Aladzhin took place, when we for the first time broke up the flanks of the " invincible " Gazi-Mukhtar Pasha. . . . Well, after the third of October we began our advance. I was commander of the advance reconnoitring division ; I had the Nizhni Novgorod dragoons, three hundred Kubantsi and a battery of horse artillery. It was a dreary country, not bad up in the mountains, beautiful, but in the hollows nothing but empty, burnt-down villages and trampled earth. On the twenty-eighth of October we descended to a valley where, by the map, there should have been a large Armenian village. Of course, there was no village left whatever, but there had been a fairly large one, and not long ago. The smoke of it was seen for many versts. I concentrated my detachment because, according to rumour, there was a powerful band of cavalry with whom we might quite possibly come into collision. I rode with the dragoons, the Cossacks going ahead. Quite close to the village the road had a sharp turn. The Cossacks galloped round and then came to a full stop, as if rooted to the earth. I galloped up to them, but before I saw with my own eyes I guessed from the smell what was the matter. The Bashi-Bazouks had left their kitchen behind. An immense waggon of fugitive Armenians had been overtaken by the ravaging enemy. The Bashi-Bazouks had made a fire under the waggon and burnt the people slowly to death. Before doing so they had bound many of the victims so that they should not escape, and had committed barbarous assaults upon them, there being many women with mutilated breasts and bodies. I could not mention all the details. One picture is clear in my eyes at this moment—a woman lying on her back on the ground, her neck and shoulders tied to the cart-wheel in such a way that she could not turn her head, and she lay there neither burnt nor broken, but with a ghastly twisted expression on her face—she had evidently died from terror. In front of her was a high pole stuck into the ground, and a naked baby was tied to it—probably her own son—all black with fire and its eyes protruding. Such a mortal sorrow overcame me that I looked upon God's earth with loathing and I acted as if I had been a machine. I gave the order for advance, and we came up to the ravaged village. It was literally razed from the earth; there was not one stone left upon another. Suddenly we saw what seemed like a scarecrow emerging from a dry well . . . all muddy and torn, he came up to us, fell flat on the ground, and began reciting something in Armenian. We made him get up, cross-questioned him, and found out that he was an

Armenian from another village. He was a little, intelligent fellow ; he had just arrived at this village when the inhabitants were beginning to flee. The fugitives had only just started on their way when the Bashi-Bazouks overtook them, a multitude of them —forty thousand, he said, but of course he didn't count them on an abacus. He concealed himself in a well. He heard the cries and so knew what was happening. Then he heard the Bashi-Bazouks turn about and gallop off. " They have probably gone to our village to do the same with our folk," said he.

When I heard that it was as if a light had suddenly shone in my soul. My heart melted, and God's world again smiled before me. " Have they long gone ? " I said to the Armenian. He reckoned— three hours.

" And is it far to your village for mounted men ? "

" About five hours."

Well, we couldn't make up three hours' difference in so short a space, that was certain. " Oh, Lord ! " said I, " isn't there another road, a shorter one ? "

" There is, there is ! There's a road through the gorge ; quite a short one. Very few people know it."

" Possible for cavalry ? "

" Yes."

" And for artillery ? "

" It would be possible, but difficult."

We gave the Armenian a horse, and with the whole detachment followed him through the gorge. How we climbed among the mountains I hardly remember. Once more I felt like a machine, though there was in my soul a lightness as if I lay on feathers.

WAR AND CHRISTIANITY

I had complete assurance. I knew what was necessary to do, and I felt what would be done.

We were just issuing from the last neck of the gorge when suddenly our Armenian gallops back, waving his arms and crying, " There they are ; there they are ! " I went ahead to a point where they were visible, and distinguished them with my glasses, a great stretch of cavalry, perhaps not forty thousand, but certainly three or four if not five thousand. The devils saw our Cossacks and turned towards us as our left flank issued from the gorge. And they began to fire on us. A gun in the hand of an Asiatic monster is pretty well as deadly as in the hands of ordinary people. We began to fall ; here and there a Cossack rolled over. The eldest of our centurions came up to me and said :

" Order us to attack, your Excellency ! Otherwise anathema will fall upon us before we get the artillery into position. Let us sweep them away ! "

" Be patient, darlings, just for a little," said I. " I know you can scatter them, but what sweetness is there in that ? God orders me to make an end of them, not to scatter them."

Well, I ordered an advance of part of our men in open formation, and they engaged the enemy, exchanging some volleys with them. We kept a hundred of the men back to mask the artillery, and placed the Nizhni Novgorods in the recesses to the left of the battery. I myself trembled all the while with impatience. The face of that burnt child with the protruding eyes was constantly before me, and our Cossacks kept falling. Oh, Lord !

LADY.—How did it end?

GENERAL.—It ended in the best way possible. The Cossacks began to retreat, crying their Cossack cries the while. The devil's brood came after them, they had got excited and had already ceased shooting. The whole crowd came galloping at us. The Cossacks rode up to within two hundred sazhens of us and then scattered, all in different directions. I saw that the hour of God's will had arrived. I ordered the dispersal of the hundred masking the battery. "All is in order; God give us His blessing!" said I to myself, and I gave the word to the artillery.

And God blessed all my six cannon. The first round put them in confusion, the whole horde turned to flight, and after the third round such a disorder arose as would take place on an ant-heap if you threw several lighted matches upon it. They went off with a rush in all directions, in many cases trampling one another down. Then our Cossacks and dragoons of the left flank went after them and cut them up like cabbage. Those who escaped the artillery perished on their swords. Many threw down their arms, leapt from their saddles, and offered themselves as hostages. But I did not interfere; they themselves knew that this was not a matter of taking hostages, and our Cossacks and Nizhni Novgorods cut them all up.

And if only these brainless devils had not taken fright at our fire, and instead of running away when they were between twenty and thirty sazhens from us had flung themselves upon us and taken the cannon, we had never given them a third round.

Well, God was with us! The business was done, and it was Easter-day in my soul, the bright day of the resurrection of Christ. We gathered our dead, thirty-seven men who had given their souls to God. We placed them on a level stretch of land in several rows, and closed their eyes. There was among us in the third hundred an old policeman, Odarchenko, a well-read man of remarkable capacity. In England he would have become Prime Minister. Now he's in Siberia for personal opposition to the authorities when they were closing some monastery of the Old Believers and destroying the grave of a much venerated elder of the sect. I called him:

"Now, Odarchenko," said I, "this is a matter of the road, and no place for deciding the right alleluias; be our priest and sing the requiem for our dead." For him that was a pleasure of the first order.

"I shall be glad to try, your Excellency," says he, his face all shining. We also found our singers for the service. We sang the departing souls away with full rites. It was impossible to get priestly permission to do such a thing, but it was not necessary: what permitted us was the word of Christ for those who lay down their life for their friends. That's how that funeral service strikes me now. The day had been a cloudy autumn one, but before sunset the heavy clouds disappeared. The gorge was black beneath us, but in the sky the light cloudlets were of many colours, as if the regiments of God were gathering. The bright festival in my soul remained. A sort of calm and incomprehensible happiness possessed me, as if all earthly impurity had been washed away, as if earthly burdens had slipped from me. I was as if in heaven. I felt the presence of God, and that only. And as Odarchenko called out the names of the newly departed warriors who had sacrificed their lives on the field of battle for faith and Tsar and fatherland, I felt that the official title given them was not merely an official verbosity, but they were indeed a Christserving army, and that war, as it was, so it is and will be to the end of the world, a great honourable and holy doing . . .

PRINCE (*after some silence*).—Well, and when you buried your people in this serene way, is it possible, however, you did not remember the enemy whom you had killed in such great numbers?

GENERAL.—No, glory be to God! We managed to move a little further back so that that carrion did not remind us of its presence.

LADY.—Ah, now you've spoilt the whole impression. How could you?

GENERAL (*turning to the Prince*).—And what would you personally have wished of me? That I should give Christian burial to these jackals who were neither Christian nor Mussulmen, but devil knows what? If I had gone out of my mind, and had indeed ordered that they be buried together with our Cossacks in one funeral service, you would very probably have convicted me of religious assault. How, man? You actually subject these dear unfortunates, who in their lifetime worshipped the devil, to a superstitious and coarse pseudo-Christian ritual! No, I had something else to do.

WAR AND CHRISTIANITY

I gave orders and made a manifesto to the effect that none of the people approach within three sazhens of this devil's carrion, for I saw that my Cossacks' fingers had long since been itching to feel their pockets according to custom. And who knew what plague might have been let loose on us! It might have been the death of us all.

PRINCE.—Have I then understood you aright? You were afraid, lest the Cossacks going to rob the bodies of the Bashi-Bazouks should carry infection into your camp?

GENERAL.—Yes, that's just what I was afraid of. It seems clear.

PRINCE.—There's your Christ-serving army!

GENERAL.—The Cossacks, eh? . . . Robbers in spirit! Always were and always will be.

PRINCE.—Are we talking in our sleep?

GENERAL.—Yes, it seems to me as if something didn't fit. I never seem to catch your drift. What were you wishing to ask?

POLITICIAN.—The Prince is probably astonished that your ideal, almost holy Cossacks, suddenly appear to be, in your own words, robbers.

PRINCE.—Yes, and I ask in what way can war be a great, honourable and holy doing when all it comes to, even by your own showing, is a struggle of one set of robbers with another.

GENERAL.—Eh! So that's what you were after—" A struggle of one set of robbers with another." Yes, there is something in what you say. I agree that it is with another set of robbers, with an altogether other set. Or do you in sober reality think that to steal when you have the chance is the same sort of thing as to roast a baby in the eyes of its mother? Now this is what I say to you. My conscience is so clear about this affair that I sometimes am sorry from the depths of my heart that I did not die at the moment when I gave the order for the last volley. I have not the slightest doubt that dying then I should have gone straight with my thirty-seven Cossacks to the Almighty, and we should have taken our places in Paradise side by side with the repentant thief of the Gospel. The story of the penitent thief is not given by chance in the Gospel.

PRINCE.—I agree; only you will certainly not find it said in the Gospel that repentant thieves are only found among people of our own nation and our own faith.

GENERAL.—When did I make any distinction of nationality or religion in this business? Are the Armenians my fellow-countrymen or fellow-Churchmen, or did I ask of what faith were this devil's brood which I destroyed with our artillery?

PRINCE.—However, you do not seem to have been able to recollect that this same devil's brood were all the same, human beings, and that in every man there is a sense of good and evil, and that every robber, be he Cossack or Bashi-Bazouk, has the chance of holding the position of the repentant thief of the Gospel.

GENERAL.—Have done with all that! First you say that an evil man is in nature like an irresponsible beast, then you say that the Bashi-Bazouk roasting a baby might turn out to be the penitent thief of the

Gospel! And you put all this forward with the one end that we should not oppose evil, even with a finger. But according to my lights, what is important is not that in every man are the roots of good and evil, but which of the two prevails. It is not so interesting that out of every kind of grape-juice it is possible to make both wine and vinegar as to know what actually is in that bottle there, wine or vinegar. Because if it is vinegar and I begin to drink it by tumblerfuls and to offer it to others under the pretext that it is made from one and the same material as wine, I shall certainly help no one by that wisdom, unless spoiling their stomachs is any help. All people are brothers. Splendid! Very glad! Yes, but what further? Brothers are of different sorts. And why not be interested to know which of my brothers is Cain and which Abel? And if before my eyes my brother Cain fall upon my brother Abel, and I then through lack of equanimity give brother Cain such a box on the ear that he's not likely to do it again,—you suddenly reproach me that I have forgotten to be brotherly. I perfectly remember why I interfered, and if I had not remembered I could quite calmly have passed by on the other side.

PRINCE.—Whence this dilemma: to pass by on the other side, or to give a box on the ear?

GENERAL.—A third way you seldom find on such occasions. You have proposed prayer to God for His direct interference, that He should instantly, and with His strong right arm, bring each devil's son to reason—though you yourself, it seems, renounce this means. But I hold that this means is good in any business and that there is no substitute. Honest folk say grace before dinner, but they chew with their own jaws. It was not without prayer that I gave the orders to the horse artillery.

PRINCE.—Such a prayer is, of course, blasphemy. It is necessary not so much to pray to God as to act according to the will of God.

GENERAL.—For instance?

PRINCE.—He who is filled with the true spirit of the Gospel will find in himself, when necessary, the power, with words and gestures and with his whole appearance to act upon the mind of his unfortunate dark brother who wishes to commit a murder or some other evil,—he will be able to make on him such a staggering impression that he will at once understand his mistake and turn away from the false road.

GENERAL.—Holy martyrs! Do you mean to say that I should have gone forward to the Bashi-Bazouks who murdered the babies, and made touching gestures and said touching words?

MR. Z.—Words, owing to the distance and to your mutual ignorance of one another's language, would, I imagine, have been completely out of place. And as far as gestures go in making a staggering impression, as you will of course, but I should have thought that under the given circumstances one couldn't think of anything better than a volley or so.

LADY.—But really, do tell us, Prince, in what language and by the help of what instruments could the General have explained himself to the Bashi-Bazouks?

PRINCE.—I did not at all mean that *they* could treat the Bashi-Bazouks according to the spirit of the Gospel. I only said that a man filled with the true spirit of the Gospel would have found the possibility on that occasion, as indeed on any other occasion, to awaken in their dark souls the good which lies hidden in every human being.

MR. Z.—You really think so?

PRINCE.—I do not doubt it in the least.

MR. Z.—And do you think that Christ was *sufficiently* penetrated by the true spirit of the Gospel, or no?

PRINCE.—What sort of a question is that?

MR. Z.—Well, this is what I'd like to know: why did not Christ bring the evangelical spirit to bear in such a way upon the souls of Judas, Herod, the Jewish Sanhedrin, and the unrepentant thief, whom commonly people forget when they speak of his repentant companion? Why did He not bring out the good in them? From a positive Christian point there is no insurmountable difficulty in it. But you have got to give up one of two things: either your habit of taking refuge with Christ and the Gospel as with the highest authority, or your moral optimism, because the third way, the well-worn way, of denying the evangelical fact itself as a modern fiction or priestly interpretation, is in the present instance completely closed to you. However you ransack the four Gospels for texts, the principal fact from the point of view of our question will remain indisputable, and that is, that Christ Himself suffered bitter persecution and death because of the malice of His enemies. That He Himself remained morally higher than all that malice, that He did not wish to offer any opposition, and that He forgave His enemies, is as comprehensible from my point of view as from yours. But why did He not, forgiving His enemies, deliver their souls from that dreadful darkness in which they then were ? Why did He not overcome their malice by the force of His own sweetness ? Why did He not awaken the sleeping good in them ? Why did He not give them light and new spiritual birth ? In a word, why did He not act upon Judas, Herod, and the Jewish Sanhedrin in the same way as He acted upon the *one* repentant thief ? Either He could not or He would not. In both instances it turns out, *according to you*, that He was not *sufficiently* penetrated with the true spirit of the Gospel, and as we are speaking, if I do not mistake, of the Gospel of Christ and not of any other gospel, it appears that Christ was not sufficiently penetrated with the true spirit of Christ— upon which result I offer you my congratulations.

PRINCE.—Oh, I am not going to enter into verbal fencing with you any more than I am going to enter into real fencing with the General, with "Christ-serving" swords . . .

(*At this point the Prince got up from his seat and wished apparently to say something very powerful, expecting with one blow, without any fencing, to overwhelm his antagonist, but at that moment it began to strike seven from a neighbouring belfry.*)

LADY.—Dinner-time ! What's more, we mustn't finish such a discussion in a hurry. After dinner we'll have our game of vint, but to-morrow we must, we absolutely must, go on with this conversation. (*To the Politician*) You agree?

POLITICIAN.—What, to continue this conversation? I was overjoyed that it had come to an end! The dispute had taken the rather unpleasant complexion of a holy war! It was too hot work for this time of the year. My health I can tell you, is dearer to me than any of these things.

LADY.—Don't pretend! You must, you absolutely must, take part. It's no use your lounging there stretched out on your deck chair like a mysterious Mephistopheles.

POLITICIAN.—Well, I might agree to take part to-morrow, but only on condition that there be less religion in it. I don't ask you to exclude it altogether, as it seems that would be impossible. Only let there be less, for God's sake, a little less!

LADY.—Your " for God's sake " is on this occasion very sweet.

MR. Z. (*to the Politician*).—The best means of making sure that there shall be less religion would be for you to speak much more, wouldn't it?

POLITICIAN.—I promise! Only to listen is, all the same, more pleasant than to talk, especially in this fine air; but for the salvation of our little circle from mutual conflict, which might possibly reflect itself in an unpleasant way in our vint, I am ready to sacrifice myself for two hours.

LADY.—Splendid! And the day after to-morrow then, we will finish this discussion about the Bible. The Prince will get ready some absolutely irrefutable argument. Only you also must be present at the end. You need a little instruction in the Scriptures.

POLITICIAN.—What! The day after to-morrow, as well? No, no! My self-sacrifice won't go as far as that. What's more, I must go to Nice the day after to-morrow.

LADY.—To Nice? What naïve diplomacy you are practising upon us! It's no good. We've long since learnt to read your cypher, and now everybody knows that when you say you're going to Nice it means you're off to Monte Carlo for a spree. Never mind, we'll manage somehow without you. Go and wallow in material things, since you're not afraid of the fact that you will have to join the world of spirits later on. Go to Monte Carlo, and may Providence reward you according to your deserts!

POLITICIAN.—My deserts don't concern Providence, as it happens, but only a little business which I have got to see through. I might try my luck with a little small change at roulette, I admit, but I shouldn't spend much.

LADY.—Only to-morrow then, we must all be present.

SECOND CONVERSATION

"*Audiatur et* altera *pars.*"

ON the following day, at the appointed hour, I met the others at afternoon tea under the palm trees. Only the Prince was absent. We had to wait for him. As I did not play cards I wrote down the whole of this conversation from the very beginning. This time the Politician spoke so much and in such a drawling way that to note down literally everything he said would be impossible. I have mentioned a sufficient number of his remarks and have endeavoured to preserve the general meaning. In many instances I can merely convey in my own words the substance of his discourses.

POLITICIAN.—I have long observed a certain peculiarity : people who have made a special hobby of some kind of higher morality cannot master the simplest and most indispensable, and according to me, the most necessary virtue—common politeness. We must therefore be grateful to the Almighty that in our midst there are comparatively few possessed of this idea of higher morality. I say *idea* advisedly, because in reality I have never met with it, nor do I believe in its existence.

LADY.—Well, that is not new, but what you say about politeness is true. Try, before you have come to the *sujet en question*, to prove that politeness is the only indispensable virtue ; try to prove it even superficially, as musical instruments are tuned before the overture begins.

POLITICIAN.—Yes, in such cases only separate sounds are heard. Such monotony would also prevail now, for scarcely anyone would care to defend another opinion before the arrival of the Prince. Besides, to speak of politeness to-day in his presence would not be quite polite.

LADY.—Certainly. And how about your argument?

POLITICIAN.—This, I think you will agree that one can exist quite well in a society where there are no chaste, disinterested or unselfish persons. I, at any rate, have got on very well in such company.

LADY.—At Monte Carlo!

POLITICIAN.—At Monte Carlo and everywhere else. In fact, nowhere is there felt to be a demand for even a single representative of the higher virtues. But try to live in a society where there is not a single polite person.

GENERAL.—I do not know to what society you are good enough to refer, but during the campaigns in Khiva and Turkey something more than politeness was needed.

POLITICIAN.—You might as well have added that for travellers in Central Africa more than politeness was required. I speak of well-organised daily life in the cultured society of human beings, and that requires none of the higher virtues or of Christianity so-called. (*Turning to Mr. Z.*) You shake your head.

MR. Z.—I recall to mind a painful incident which was told me.

LADY.—And what was that?
MR. Z.—My friend N. died quite suddenly.
GENERAL.—The well-known novelist?
MR. Z.—The same.
POLITICIAN.—The newspapers wrote rather mysteriously about his death.
MR. Z.—Precisely—very mysteriously.
LADY.—But what made you think of him just now? Did he die from somebody's lack of politeness?
MR. Z.—On the contrary, merely from his own exaggerated politeness.
GENERAL.—And even on this point we do not appear to agree.
LADY.—If possible, tell us all about it.
MR. Z.—There is nothing to hide. My friend, who also thought that politeness, although not the only virtue, was, at all events, the most necessary step in social morality, considered it his bounden duty to fulfil all its dictates. Among the duties which he imposed on himself was that of reading all letters addressed to him, even from unknown people, as well as books and pamphlets for review. He read all the letters and noticed all the books. He conscientiously carried out every request addressed to him, and consequently was busy all day with other people's affairs, while his own occupied him at night. What is more, he accepted all invitations and received all comers. While my friend was young and could stand strong drinks the hard labour imposed by politeness, although undermining his health, did not degenerate into tragedy. Wine cheered his heart and saved him from despair.

Sometimes, when ready to seize a rope with which to hang himself, he stretched out his hand for the bottle, and that gave him courage. Constitutionally he was weak, and at the age of forty-five he had to give up strong drink. When sober, this slavery seemed hell to him, and now, I am informed, he has committed suicide.

LADY.—What! And simply from politeness? But he was mad!

MR. Z.—No doubt he lost his reason, but I venture to think that word " simply " is not applicable to this case.

GENERAL.—I have also seen similar cases of insanity, and if one tried to fathom them one might also go mad. It is far from simple.

POLITICIAN.—In every case it is clear that politeness has nothing to do with the matter. The Spanish throne was no more to blame for the madness of the *chinovnik* Poprischin [1] than the necessity to be polite was answerable for your friend's insanity.

MR. Z.—Of course, I am not against politeness, but only against making a law of politeness.

POLITICIAN.—Absolute rules, as everything absolute, are merely the inventions of people bereft of common sense and of the feeling of living reality. I do not admit any absolute rules, I only accept *indispensable* rules. For instance, I am well aware that if I do not adopt the rule of cleanliness the result will be unpleasant to myself and to others. In order not to experience unpleasant sensations, I adhere unalterably to the rule of washing myself every day, to

[1] In Gogol's "Diary of a Madman."

putting on clean linen, etc., not because it is a generally received custom of other people or myself, or because it is a sacred duty, or a sin to neglect it, but merely because uncleanliness, *ipso facto*, is a material inconvenience. Just the same applies to politeness, of which cleanliness is a component part. For me and for others it is much more *convenient* to perform than to neglect the rules of politeness, and therefore I adhere to them. Your friend imagined that politeness meant answering all letters and executing all requests without reference to convenience and personal advantage ; that was not politeness, but a kind of foolish self-sacrifice.

MR. Z.—Morbid development of conscientiousness became, in his case, a mania, which killed him.

LADY.—But it is awful that a man should perish through such nonsense. Could not you bring him to reason ?

MR. Z.—I did my best, and was even assisted by a pilgrim from Mount Athos, who was half crazy, but a very remarkable person. My friend greatly respected him and often consulted him in spiritual matters. That man struck at once at the root of the trouble. I knew the pilgrim well and was often present at the discussions.

When my friend began telling him about his moral doubts, saying—was he right in this or had he sinned in that, Varsonophia sharply interrupted him : " Eh, why are you grieving about your sins— don't! Listen to me: sin five hundred and thirty-nine times in a day, but don't grieve about it ; that's the chief thing. If to sin is evil, then to remember sin is evil. There is nothing worse than to call to mind one's own sins. Better think of the evil which others do to you, there is some use in that; for the future you will beware of such persons. As for your evil actions—forget them, so that they may disappear altogether. There is only one deadly sin and that is despondency. From despondency comes despair; and that is more than sin, it is spiritual death. Well, and what other sins are there? How about drunkenness? A sensible man drinks when he is thirsty; he does not drink at random, but a fool gorges himself even with plain water, therefore the evil is not in the wine, but in the foolishness. Some people in their foolishness burn their insides with *vodka*, and even their outsides turn black and sparks fly about. I have seen it with my own eyes. It is something worse than sin when the fiery Gehenna pierces through the skin. As regards all the various violations of the seventh commandment, I will speak according to my conscience: it is difficult to judge and impossible to praise! I do not recommend it! There is no denying it is a thrilling pleasure, but it leads to sorrow and shortens life. If you don't believe me, see here what a learned German doctor writes." And Varsonophia took an antiquated-looking book from the shelf and began turning over its leaves. " Here is Hufland. See page 176." And he read sententiously how the German author warns against the foolish waste of vital power. " Well, you see, why should a reasonable man exhaust his strength? In early, reckless years evil is done and health is lost. But to recall all the past and be distressed, saying why did I lose my innocence, my purity of soul and body, that is sheer nonsense ; it is simply playing the buffoon to the devil. Of course it flatters the devil that your soul should not rise higher, but remain in the same dirty slum. Here is my advice : When the devil begins to trouble about all this repentance, just spit upon him and say ' Here are all my heavy sins, they are not very important.' I promise he will leave you in peace ! I speak from experience. . . . And for what other infractions of the law are you responsible ? You wouldn't steal ? And if you did there is no great harm ; nowadays everyone steals. It follows you mustn't worry about these trifles, but only beware of being despondent. When thoughts come about sins—have not I wronged or offended some one ?— go to the theatre, or to some merry friends, or read some funny stories. And if a rule is wanted, here it is : be firm in belief, not from fear of sin, but because it is very pleasant for a wise man to live with God, for without God life is bad. Study the word of God, for if you read with attention every line is worth a rouble ; pray earnestly once or twice a day. Don't forget to wash yourself, and sincere prayer is even better for the soul than soap for the body. Fast for thy stomach's sake and thy other internal organs; doctors advise fasting after forty. Don't think about other people's affairs or trouble about philanthropy, if you have work to do ; give money to beggars not counting it ; give donations to churches and monasteries without stint ; it will be recorded in heaven, and you will be healthy in soul and body. Avoid bigots who like to pry into other people's souls, because their own souls are empty."

Such speeches produced a favourable influence on my friend, but they could not drive away the ideas which pressed on his mind, and latterly he seldom saw Varsonophia.

POLITICIAN.—The pilgrim says, in substance, pretty much what I do.

LADY.—So much the better. Really, what a wonderful moralist! Sin but don't repent—I like that very much.

GENERAL.—I presume he does not say the same to everybody. If it were a murderer or a blackguard I suppose he would give some different teaching.

MR. Z.—Well, of course. But when he meets moral, scrupulous people he instantly becomes a philosopher and even a fatalist. A very clever and well-educated old lady was delighted with him. Although of the Russian orthodox faith, she had been educated abroad. She heard much about Varsonophia and consulted him as though he were a *directeur de conscience,* but he did not give her a chance of saying much about such *trash!* "Who wants it?" said he. "Why even I, a common moujik, find it tedious to listen to you, and do you think that it can interest God Almighty! And what is there to talk about! You are old and weak and never will be any better!" She told me this with laughter and tears in her eyes. Still, she tried to refute it, though he finally convinced her by a story about an old hermit. Varsonophia also often spoke to me and to N. about this hermit. Not a bad story, but too long to relate at present.

LADY.—But tell it to us in a few words.

MR. Z.—I will try. In the desert of Nitria two hermits were " working out " their salvation. Their caves were not far from each other, but they never conversed, only chanted psalms occasionally. Thus they passed many years, and their fame began to spread through Egypt and the neighbouring countries. But in course of time the devil succeeded in poisoning their souls; they packed their belongings, their baskets and beds of palm leaves and branches, and marched off to Alexandria. There they sold their work, and on the money they got for it they spent three days and three nights with drunkards and sinners and then returned to their desert. One of them lamented and cried most bitterly: " I am lost and accursed ! Such madness and evil doings can never be forgiven. All my fastings, vigils and prayers are wasted."

The other pilgrim walked beside him and sang psalms joyfully to himself. The first cried:

" Are you mad ? "

" Why ? " asked the joyful one.

" Aren't you sorry ? "

" About what should I be sorry ? "

" And about Alexandria ? "

" Glory be to the Almighty, who preserves the famous and God-fearing city."

" And what did we do at Alexandria ? "

" Of course we sold our baskets, bowed low to St. Mark and visited the other temples ; we waited on the pious protector of the city, we conversed with the virtuous matron Leonilla . . ."

"Did not we spend the night in a house of ill-fame?"

"God preserve us! The evening and night we passed in the patriarch's hostelry."

"Holy martyrs! Why he is off his head. . . . And was it not there that we were filled with wine?"

"We tasted wine and food from the patriarch's hospitable board on the occasion of the Presentation of the Blessed Virgin in the Temple."

"Wretched man! And who kissed us, to say nothing worse? . . ."

"And at parting we received a holy kiss from that holy father of fathers, the blessed Archbishop of Alexandria and of all Egypt; yes, and of Libya and of Pentapolis and of Kur-Timothee with its spiritual court, and with all the fathers and brothers of his divinely appointed clergy."

"But are you mocking me? Or has the devil possessed you after yesterday's evil deeds? You, cursed man, have embraced sinners!"

"Well, I do not know into whom the devil has entered: into me who rejoice in the gifts of God and in the kindness extended to us by the heads of the Church, and praise the Creator with all creation, or into you, who rave and call the house of our blessed father and pastor a house of ill-fame, and defame the God-loving clergy, calling them sinners, as it were!"

"Oh, thou heretic! Aryan offspring, cursed lips of Apollonion!"

The hermit, afflicted by his sinful transgressions, threw himself on his companion and began beating him with all his might. After this they went in silence to their caves.

The despondent hermit filled the desert with lamentations, groans and sobs, beating his head against the stone floor. In the morning a new idea occupied his mind : " By many years of good deeds I earned the special blessing of the Holy Ghost, which has already appeared in signs and wonders. But *after that*, by lowering myself to carnal lusts, I sinned against the Holy Ghost, and that sin, according to the word of God, will not be forgiven in this world or the next. I cast the pearl of heavenly purity before swine, *i.e.*, before devils, who, treading on it, will turn and rend me. But if in any case I am lost for ever, what have I to do in the desert ? "

And he went to Alexandria and led a loose life. When in want of money he joined himself to other dissolute revellers, killing and robbing a rich merchant. The crime was discovered, he was taken to the town court, condemned to death, and he died without repentance. Meanwhile, his former companion, continuing his asceticism, attained the highest Church dignities and was renowned for wonderful deeds. At his word even barren women bore male children. When the day of his death came his shrivelled and dried up body suddenly became young and beautiful, it shone and perfumed the ambient air. A monastery was erected over his wonder-working body, and his name passed from the Church in Alexandria to Byzantium, and thence to the shrines of Kiev and Moscow. "The lesson of this story," said Varsono, "is that all sins are harmless except despondency. The two men committed every iniquity conjointly, but only one of them perished, namely, he who desponded."

GENERAL.—You see, monks must have a courageous spirit, but nowadays even soldiers are discouraged.

MR. Z.—It seems we have drifted from the question of politeness, but have returned to our principal subject.

LADY.—And here comes the Prince. How are you? In your absence we have been speaking about politeness.

PRINCE.—Please excuse me, I could not get away earlier. I received a lot of papers and printed matter from our friends. I will show them to you later on.

LADY.—And I will afterwards tell you a holy anecdote, which entertained us in your absence. It was about two monks. But now it is the turn of our Monte Carloist to speak. Well, let us know what he has to say about war after yesterday's conversation.

POLITICIAN.—From yesterday's conversation I remember the reference to Vladimir Monomakh, and the General's military story. Let this be the starting point for the further discussion of the question. It is impossible to deny that Vladimir Monomakh did well when he defeated the Poloftsi, and that the General did his duty when he destroyed the Bashi-Bazouks

Lady.—That means that you agree.

Politician.—I agree with what I have had the honour of telling you, namely, that Monomakh and the General acted in the way they were bound to do in *the given situation ;* but how are we to appreciate that situation, or to justify the perpetuation of war and militarism ?

Prince.—That is precisely what I say.

Lady.—And the United States ?

Politician.—I thank you for the happy example. I speak of the creation of a *State*. Of course, the United States, as a European *colony*, was founded as all other colonies, not by war, but by navigation. However, as soon as that colony desired to be a State, it had to obtain its political independence by a lengthy war.

Prince.—Because a State is created by war, which certainly cannot be denied, you evidently conclude that war is important, while I conclude that it proves the unimportance of the State. I mean, of course, for people who have refused to bow down to brute force.

Politician.—And why do you speak of worshipping brute force ? Try to organise a sound community of human beings without Government control, then only can you discuss the non-importance of Governments. Until then, the State and all that you and I owe it, remains an established fact, while your attacks are mere insignificant words. Therefore, I repeat : the great historical meaning of war, as the principal condition in the foundation of a State, is beside the question. But I ask : Must we not consider the great business of forming an Empire as already accomplished in substance? Details can, of course, be arranged even without such heroic measures as war. In ancient times and in the Middle Ages, when the European world of culture was but an island in the middle of an ocean of barbarism, military organisation was necessary for self-preservation. People had to be always in readiness to drive away wild hordes, which came from unknown regions to crush dawning civilisation. And now only the non-European elements should be termed islands, while European culture has become the ocean which surrounds them. Our men of science, our adventurers and missionaries have scoured the whole terrestrial globe and have discovered no serious danger to the culture of the world. Wild tribes are very successfully destroying themselves and are dying out; warlike barbarians, as, for instance, Turks and Japanese, are becoming civilised and are losing their militarism. Meanwhile, the unification of European nations in general cultural life . . .

LADY (*under her breath*).—Monte Carlo.

POLITICIAN (*continuing his oration*).—has been so strengthened that fighting between those nations assumes the character of civil war. It would be unpardonable in every respect, since there is a possibility of arranging international quarrels peaceably. To settle disputes by fighting would at the present time be as fantastic as to go from Petersburg to Marseilles in a sailing vessel or in a Russian *tarantass* drawn by three horses. I fully

WAR AND CHRISTIANITY 55

admit, however, that the ancient modes of travel described by Pushkin and Lermontof are much more poetical than the whistle of a steamer or the cry " *en voiture, messieurs.*" I am equally prepared to admit the æsthetic superiority of " bristling steel " and of brilliant regiments over the negotiations of diplomats and their peaceful congresses. But the serious consideration of a question, treating of life and death, must ignore æsthetic beauty, which has nothing in common with war. I do assure you that it is in no way beautiful, as represented by the fancy of the poet or the artist. When it is understood that war, with all its attractive interest for poets and painters, is useless, because unprofitable, *then the military period of history must end.* I, of course, speak in general—*en grand.* There cannot be a question of immediate disarmament, but I am firmly convinced that neither we nor our children will ever witness great wars, real European wars. As for our grandchildren, they will only read in historical works of little wars somewhere in Asia and Africa.

My reply concerning Vladimir Monomakh is as follows : When it became necessary to protect the future of the newly-born Russian State from the inroads of Poloftsi, Tartars, etc., war was the most indispensable and important business. The same may, to a certain extent, be said about the epoch of Peter the Great, when it was necessary to guarantee the future of Russia as a *European* power. But after that the meaning of war becomes more and more an exploded question, and at present, as already stated, the military period in Russia, and elsewhere, is a thing of the past. What I have just said about our own country is applicable—certainly, *mutatis mutandis* — to other European States. Formerly, war was everywhere the principal and unavoidable means for the protection and security of government and of national existence. When that is once attained war will lose its *raison d'être* and cease to exist.

I may add that I am astonished at the way some modern philosophers discuss the *meaning of war* with reference to the times. Has war any meaning ? *C'est selon.* Yesterday war had significance everywhere ; to-day somewhere, perhaps in Africa or Central Asia, where wild tribes still exist ; to-morrow it will have no meaning anywhere. It is remarkable that in proportion to losing its practical meaning, war also loses, slowly but surely, its mystical aureole. It is even evident among the masses of a nation as backward as our own. Judge for yourselves : only the other day the General triumphantly pointed out that our saints were either monks or soldiers. But I ask you : to what special historical epoch does all this military sanctity or saintly militarism belong ? Does it not form part of that period when war was *really* unavoidable, beneficial, and, if you will, holy doing ? Our saintly warriors were all princes of the Kiev and Tartar epoch. But among them I do not remember any lieutenant-generals or other generals. What does that mean ? Take two eminent warriors with equal claims to sanctity : the one is considered a saint and the other is not. Why, may I ask, is

Alexander Nevsky, who beat the Livonians and the Swedes in the thirteenth century, a saint, and why is Alexander Suvorof, who beat the French in the eighteenth century, not a saint? Suvorof could not be reproached with want of sanctity. He was sincerely religious, sang in choirs, read from the *ambon*, and led an unblemished life. He had no love intrigues, and even his religious *naïveté* would rather be an argument in favour of canonisation. But the point is, that Alexander Nevsky fought for the national-political future of his country, which was already partly crushed by inroads from the East, and could scarcely withstand the invasions from the West. The instinctive common sense of the people understood the vital importance of the situation and conferred on their Prince the highest recompense they could devise, canonisation. Suvorof's exploits, although incomparably more important in a military sense, especially his crossing the Alps, which was worthy of Hannibal, were absolutely necessary to save Russia from annihilation. Therefore he is merely a military celebrity.

LADY.—But the leaders of the army who fought Napoleon in the year 1812 were not canonised, although they did save Russia.

POLITICIAN.—The expression saving Russia from Napoleon is patriotic rhetoric. He would not have devoured us, nor did he intend to do so. That we finally overcame him certainly shows our national Imperial power and raises our sentiments of patriotism. But that the war of the year 1812 was called forth by some unavoidable necessity—that I can never admit! It might have been quite possible to come to terms with Napoleon instead of provoking war. Although the venture turned out successfully and the end of the war flattered our national vanity, the result can scarcely be admitted to have been beneficial. If two strong men fall out, without rhyme or reason, and the one overpowers the other, not without injuring their health, I might call the victor a fine fellow! But the necessity of having such an exhibition remains a riddle for me. The glory of the year 1812, and the display of national heroism at that time, whatever might have been the cause of the war, are inexplicable. A poet calls it a "holy event." That is all very fine as far as poetry goes, but I look at the outcome of this "event" and behold the Archimandrite Photius, Magnitzky and Arakcheef on the one hand, and on the other the conspiracy of the Dekabrists—*i.e.*, thirty years of the regime of belated militarism which brought about the defeat at Sevastopol.

LADY.—And Pushkin?

POLITICIAN.—Pushkin? . . . Why Pushkin?

LADY.—I read the other day in the newspapers that the national poetry of Pushkin was created by the military glory of the year 1812.

MR. Z.—Not without the special participation of the artillery, as is apparent from the poet's name.[1]

POLITICIAN.—It may be so. But to continue. As time advanced, the uselessness, the unprofitableness of our wars become more clearly evident. The Crimean War is thought much of among us, because

[1] *Pushka* in Russian is a gun.

it is supposed that its unsuccessful termination occasioned the liberation of the serfs and other reforms of Alexander II. If that is so, then the good results of an *unsuccessful* war, precisely because it is unsuccessful, do not exactly constitute an apology for war in general. If I, for no good reason, jump off a balcony and dislocate my hand, and should this accident prevent me from signing a wasteful bill of exchange, I should be pleased with what happened. But I will not maintain that it is necessary to jump off a balcony instead of walking down the staircase. If your head is not injured, it is not necessary for you to get a damaged hand in order to prevent you from attaching your signature to a ruinous transaction. The same common sense that will preserve you from jumping off balconies will also preserve you from signing bills foolishly. I think that without the Crimean War the reforms of the Emperor Alexander II. would have probably been introduced, and perhaps in a more comprehensive and sounder manner. I shall not go on proving this thesis any further, but will return to our subject. In any case, political actions cannot be valued by unforeseen consequences. The very beginning of the Crimean War, *i.e.*, the attack of our army on the Danube in 1853, cannot be reasonably justified. I cannot call a policy sound which one day protects Turkey from the invasion of the Egyptian Pasha, Mehmet Ali, contrary to our interests, and the next day prepares the destruction of the same Turkey, which it has saved and strengthened, to say nothing of having risked a quarrel with the Anglo-French coalition. This is no policy, but a kind of Don Quixotism in connection with our last Turkish campaign. I hope the General will pardon me.

LADY.—And how about the Bashi-Bazouks, whom the General destroyed with your full approbation.

POLITICIAN.—I crave pardon. I maintain that, at the present time, war has become *useless*, and the General's recent story is the best illustration of this truth. I understand that when one is in duty bound to participate in war and one meets irregular Turkish troops, guilty of outrageous cruelties against peaceful inhabitants (*he looks at the Prince*), then every man not bound by " absolute principles " must destroy the transgressors without mercy, as the General has done. He cannot then think about their moral regeneration as suggested by the Prince. But I beg leave to ask, firstly, who was the real cause of all these atrocities, and, secondly, what has been accomplished by armed intervention? According to my conscience, I must reply to the first question by merely exposing the bad military policy, which, while exciting the passions and pretensions of the Turkish *rajas*, mocked the Turks. It must be admitted that the Bulgarian atrocities only commenced when Bulgaria was infested with revolutionary committees, and the Turks were alarmed by the possibility of foreign intervention and the breaking up of Turkey. The same thing happened in Armenia. As regards the second question, what was achieved by intervention? The answer is given by the latest events and is so obvious that everyone can see it. In 1877 our General destroys several thousand Bashi-Bazouks, saving *perhaps* thereby several hundred Armenians. In 1895, in the same locality, similar Bashi-Bazouks murder not hundreds but thousands of the inhabitants. If we are to credit various correspondents (although I do not advise you to believe them), nearly half a million of men were cut to pieces. Well, this may be a fable. However, in any case the Armenian murders were on a considerably greater scale than the Bulgarian atrocities. And these are the beneficent results of our patriotic and philanthropic wars.

GENERAL.—Who can understand this? Here bad politics are to blame and there a patriotic war. One might suppose that Gorchakof and Giers were soldiers, or that Disraeli and Bismarck were Russian patriots and philanthropists!

POLITICIAN.—Is it possible that my statements are not clear? I have in view a definite connection, not abstract or ideal, but an entirely real, pragmatic connection between the war of 1877, which was itself a result of our bad politics, and of the recent atrocities in Armenia. You may perhaps be aware, or, if not, it may be useful for you to know, what happened after 1878. Turkey saw from the treaty of San Stefano what awaited her in the future in Europe and decided to guarantee its existence at all events in Asia. First of all, Turkey made sure of England's support at the Berlin Congress; but to be on the safe side, the Turkish Government set about organising and strengthening its regular army in Armenia, *i.e.*, increasing the number of those "devils" with whom the General had to deal. This proved to be a good move, because some fifteen years after Disraeli had guaranteed to Turkey the possession of its Asiatic dominions[1] in exchange for the cession of Cyprus, circumstances changed. English policy became anti-Turkish and pro-Armenian; English agitators appeared in Armenia, just as formerly Slavophil agitators had penetrated into Bulgaria. It was then that those "devils," as the General calls them, became the *men of the situation* and devoured the lion's share of Christian flesh.

GENERAL.—I cannot listen to you saying such things! What war was to blame in this case? Fear God, my friend. If in 1878 statesmen had accomplished their work as satisfactorily as the soldiers did theirs, there would have been no question of strengthening and organising Turkish irregular troops in Armenia, and consequently no atrocities would have been perpetrated.

POLITICIAN.—That means, you suggest, the final destruction of the Turkish Empire?

GENERAL.—Yes! Although I like and respect the Turks with all my heart, especially when I compare them with all the mongrel Ethiopians. At the same time I think it is necessary to make an end of the Turkish Empire.

POLITICIAN.—I also should have nothing against this, provided your so-called Ethiopians could organise some kind of an empire of their own. The fact is, they only know how to fight among them-

---

[1] On the understanding that reforms should be introduced in Armenia, which Turkey did not do.

selves, and the Turkish Government is as indispensable for them as the presence of Turkish troops is necessary in Jerusalem for the maintenance of the peace and well-being of the Christian sects.

LADY.—I quite expected that you were prepared to give Our Lord's Sepulchre to the Turks.

POLITICIAN.—And you probably think that such is the case in consequence of my being godless or callous? Meanwhile in reality I desire to retain the Turks in Jerusalem in consequence of the small but inextinguishable spark of religious sentiment which remains in me from my childhood. I know to a certainty that when the Turkish soldiers are removed from Jerusalem, the Christians there will murder each other even before the Holy Sanctuary is destroyed. In case my impressions and conclusions strike you as suspicious, ask some pilgrims whom you can trust, or, what is better still, go there yourself and see things with your own eyes.

LADY.—Go to Jerusalem? Certainly not! What more could I see by going there myself? No, I am afraid!

POLITICIAN.—Now we have the reason.

LADY.—How strange. You disagree with the General, but both of you praise the Turks.

POLITICIAN.—The General probably values them as good soldiers, whereas I approve of them as the guardians of peace and order in the East.

LADY.—Fine peace and order—to murder tens of thousands of people! Better tolerate disorder.

POLITICIAN.—As I have already explained, the

slaughter was provoked by revolutionary agitation. Why should one demand from the Turks the elevated Christian sentiments of charity and mercy which are not demanded from any other nations, be it even Christians ? Please name any country where an armed rising has been quelled without cruel and arbitrary measures. I am ready to admit that the Turkish Government overdid it, like Ivan IV., when he drowned ten thousand peaceful citizens of Novgorod, or as the commissaries of the French Convention with their *noyades* and *fusillades* or as the English in India when they crushed the mutiny in 1857. All the same, there is no doubt, if the various co-religionaries and Ethiopians, as the General terms them, were left to their own devices, there would be more carnage than under Turkish rule.

GENERAL.—But do I suggest to put the Ethiopians in the place of the Turks ? The matter is simple : we should take Constantinople and Jerusalem and make them Russian provinces, under military rule, as in Samarkand or Ashabad. The Turks, when they lay down their arms, might be satisfied and indemnified as regards their religion and in other respects.

POLITICIAN.—Well, I trust you are not speaking seriously, otherwise I should have reason to doubt . . . your patriotism. If we had begun the war with similar radical intentions it would probably have again provoked a European conflict. Ultimately your Ethiopians would have joined the hostile coalition in order to obtain their emancipation. They understand very well that under Russian rule they would not be very free to show " their national physiognomy," as the Bulgarians say. Instead of the destruction of Turkey another sack of Sevastopol, *en grand,* would be repeated. Although we have often been guilty of political incompetence, I am sure that such madness as a new war with Turkey will not occur. But if it did happen, every patriot would have to cry out in despair about Russia: *quem Deus vult perdere, prius dementat.*

LADY.—Evidently history is not made to your liking. You are probably as much for Austria as for Turkey?

POLITICIAN.—On that question it is needless for me to expatiate, because more competent people— the national leaders of Bohemia—have long ago declared : " If Austria had not existed it would have been necessary to invent her." The recent parliamentary conflicts in Vienna serve as good illustrations of this aphorism, and present a picture in miniature of what would happen in those countries on the disappearance of the Hapsburg dynasty.

LADY.—And what have you to say about the Franco-Russian alliance ? Somehow, you appear to be reticent on that score.

POLITICIAN.—Yes, I do not intend now to enter into the details of that delicate question. In general I may say that a *rapprochement* with a progressive and wealthy nation like France is in every case to our interest. Besides, this alliance is an alliance of peace and a precaution—thus, at least, it is considered in high quarters, where it was concluded and is maintained.

Mr. Z.—The question of moral and cultural advantages emanating from the *rapprochement* of the two nations is a complicated matter and is not clear to me. But in joining one of the two inimical camps on the continent of Europe, do we not lose politically the advantage of our independent position as possible arbiters? By joining one side we equalise the relative strength of both coalitions, but do we not thereby create the possibility of a military collision? France by herself could not fight against the Triple Alliance, but with Russia's aid she might.

Politician.—What you observe would be perfectly correct if somebody was interested to kindle a European war, but nobody desires to do that. And in any case it is much easier for Russia to confirm France in the way of peace than it would be for France to entice Russia into war. Both restraint of France and temptation of us are undesirable. It is, however, most satisfactory that contemporary nations not only do not desire war, but are forgetting how to fight.

Take the latest collision, the Spanish-American war. Well, what kind of a war was that? A doll's comedy, a fight in a Punch and Judy show! "After a protracted and murderous war the enemy fell back, having had one man killed and two wounded. We had no losses." Or again: "The whole of the enemy's fleet, after desperate opposition, surrendered unconditionally to our cruiser. 'Money enough.' There were no casualties on either side." The whole war appears to have been carried on on similar lines. I am astonished that people are not more

WAR AND CHRISTIANITY

struck by this new character of war, by its bloodless nature. This transformation came about under our very eyes. We all remember what *bulletins* were issued in 1870 and 1877.

GENERAL.—Don't anticipate events, for when two really military nations come into collision you will soon see what *bulletins* will be issued.

POLITICIAN.—I don't think so. It is not long since Spain was a first-class military nation. It strikes me that in humanity, as in the human body, organs which are not wanted become atrophied; military qualities are not wanted, so they begin to disappear. And if they were to reappear, I should be as much astonished as to see a bat with eagle's eyes or men with tails.

LADY.—And how is it that you have been praising Turkish soldiers?

POLITICIAN.—I praised them as guardians of internal order in a State. In that sense military power or, as it is styled, the " military hand," *manus militaris*, will long be needed, but that is no impediment to the disappearance of militarism.

The desire and means for carrying on international wars, the outcome of national *pugnacity*, is disappearing. It degenerates into parliamentary wrangles. Such a state of things will probably continue as long as opposing parties and opinions exist. To control them the *manus militaris* is indispensable, even when wars—international or internecine—are merely an historical reminiscence.

GENERAL.—What you say means that you compare the police to the *coccyx* which remains in man after his legendary tail has disappeared. That may be witty, but are you not too hasty in comparing us soldiers to the vanished tail? Because some nations have degenerated and have lost their prowess, is that a proof that military instincts have disappeared from the whole world? Perhaps by some of your "measures" and "systems" the Russian soldier might be converted into a *jelly*, but I venture to think that God Almighty will spare us.

LADY (*turning to Politician*).—But you have not explained by what means, without war, historical questions, like the Eastern, are to be settled! If Eastern Christians seeking independence are slaughtered by Turks, are we to look on with folded hands? Admitting that you justly criticised former wars, I will repeat the words of the Prince, although not in the same sense as he used them: What are we to do if atrocities recommence?

POLITICIAN.—We must collect our wits before these atrocities begin, and instead of our bad policy adopt a good one, be it even German: not provoking the Turks, and not shouting in an inebriated condition that the Cross must be replaced on St. Sophia.

For our mutual interest we should conciliate Turkey in a quiet and friendly manner. It rests with us to convince the Turks that slaughtering the population is not only a bad but a very unprofitable operation.

MR. Z.—In such admonitions, combined with railway concessions and other commercial and industrial enterprises, the Germans will be sure to anticipate us, and to vie with them would be hopeless.[1]

POLITICIAN.—There is no question of vying! If some one else takes on heavy work instead of me, surely it is only for me to rejoice and be grateful. But if, on the contrary, I am angry because he did it and not I, such anger would be unworthy of a true man. It would be equally unworthy for a nation like Russia to be the dog in the manger. If others can accomplish the good work quicker and better than we can, it would be to our advantage. I ask you, why did we wage war against Turkey in the nineteenth century if not to protect the rights of Turkish Christians? And what does it signify if the Germans attain the same object by peaceful means, by *culture*? If in 1895 the Germans had been as firmly established in Asiatic Turkey as the English in Egypt there would certainly have been no complaints about Armenian atrocities.

LADY.—So you also want to put an end to Turkey, but you somehow desire that it should be Germany who should devour her?

POLITICIAN.—I admire the wisdom of German policy, for the very reason that it does not want to devour indigestible objects. Germany's policy is more artful: to introduce Turkey into the concert of civilised nations and to assist the Turks to educate themselves. This *modus operandi* would enable them

[1] These words, written by me in October, 1899, were confirmed a month later by the German-Turkish convention concerning matters in Asia Minor and the Bagdad railway.—V. S.

to govern justly and humanely those nationalities which, in consequence of their mutual antagonism, cannot manage their own affairs in a peaceful manner.

LADY.—You are quite a story teller! Is it possible to put a Christian nation under Turkish rule for all time? I admire the Turks in many respects; but all the same, they are barbarians, and their last word will always be brute force. European civilisation will only make them worse.

POLITICIAN.—The same and even more might have been said about Russia under Peter the Great. We remember "Turkish atrocities," but was it long ago that in Russia and in other countries atrocities disappeared? "Miserable Christians groaning under the Mussulman yoke." And is it long since Christians, not pagans, in Russia groaned under the yoke of bad serf owners? What about those who in those days suffered cruel corporal punishment? Still, a fair answer to these groans of Russian Christians was the abolition of serfdom and of barbarous corporal punishment, and not the destruction of Russia. Why, therefore, should the reply to Bulgarian and Armenian atrocities be necessarily the destruction of Turkey, where these groans are heard but may be prevented?

LADY.—It is not the same thing when disorders take place in Christian countries, where they can easily be set right, as when a Christian nation is oppressed by non-Christians.

POLITICIAN.—The alleged impossibility of reorganising Turkey is merely hostile prejudice, as the Germans have proved. They also helped to dispel the prejudice that the Russians were by nature barbarians. As regards your Christians and non-Christians the *victims* of various brutalities—*la question manque d'intérêt*. If a man tries to murder me, I do not say, my dear sir, what is your religion? And it would be no consolation to me if the murderers were Christians who broke God's laws. Is it not evident that the Christianity of Ivan IV., or of the woman Soltikova, or of Arakcheef is no advantage, and that their life is characterised by wickedness which in other religions would be almost impossible? Yesterday the General spoke about the crimes of the wild Kurds, and mentioned, in passing, their devil-worship. Certainly it is very wicked to roast infants and grown-up persons on a slow fire, and I am prepared to call such deeds devilish. It is, however, well known that Ivan IV. had a partiality for roasting people on slow fires, and that he even stirred the coals with his staff. And he was not a barbarian nor a devil-worshipper, but an intellectual and learned man of his generation. What is more, he was versed in Holy Writ and in the tenets of Orthodoxy. But are not the Bulgarian Stambulov, or the Serbian Milan, rather Turks than representatives of so-called Christian nations? It would appear that your "Christianity" is an empty word.

Lady.—Such judgment would come naturally from the Prince.

Politician.—When it is a question of a self-evident truth I am not only in sympathy with our highly-respected Prince but even with Balaam's ass.

Mr. Z.—Your Excellency in kindly taking a

leading part in our conversation did not, I presume, entertain the intention of discussing Christianity or Biblical animals. Even at the present moment there still sounds in my ear your heart's cry of yesterday: " Only less religion, for God's sake ! " That being so, would you kindly return to the subject and solve my difficulty ? You justly observed that we must not destroy the Turkish Empire, but civilise it. You also stated that Germany is much more fitted to civilise the Turks than we are. In that case, what is our Russian function in the Eastern Question ?

POLITICIAN.—In what ? I should have thought it was clear, we have no function. Under the title of a special function of Russian policy you, of course, understand that Russia should herself solve the problem, in opposition to the aspirations of all the other European nations. But I may tell you that such a policy has never existed. We have deviated, for instance, in the fifties and the seventies, from this plan, but those sad deviations are precisely what I term bad politics, unpleasant results.

Speaking in general, Russian policy in the Eastern Question cannot be considered personal or isolated. Her problem, from the sixteenth and even to the end of the eighteenth century, consisted in protecting the civilised world, conjointly with Poland and Austria, from the threatened Turkish invasion. This defensive measure (even without a formal alliance) rendered it necessary to act together with the Poles, the Austrians and the Venetian Republic. It was a general policy and not the policy of any single State. At the present time this general agreement remains unchanged, although the aim and means of action have had to be altered. Now, it is not a question of protecting Europe against Turkish barbarity, but of converting Turkey into a European State. To attain the former object military action was required, but now peaceful measures are wanted. But in all cases the problem remains the same. Formerly there was solidarity among the European nations in military defence, now there is solidarity in spreading civilisation and culture.

GENERAL.—However, the former military solidarity in Europe did not prevent Richelieu and Louis XIV. from concluding an alliance with Turkey against the Hapsburgs.

POLITICIAN.—It was a bad Bourbon policy, which, combined with their foolish internal politics, was condemned, as it deserved, by history.

LADY.—You call it history : I believe it used to be termed *regicide*.

MR. Z.—But that exactly means *wicked* history.

POLITICIAN (*turning to the Lady*).—The fact is that no political mistake remains unpunished. Those who like may discover something mystical in it, but I see nothing of the kind. If I were to give up *soured milk*, which suits me now, and went in for champagne as before, the *ancien régime* would kill me as it did the Bourbons.

LADY.—But you will agree that your *soured milk* policy becomes as wearisome as the Bourbons.

POLITICIAN (*offended*).—If I were not interrupted,

I would long ago have exhausted the question and made room for a more entertaining speaker.

LADY.—Well, well, don't be offended. I was only joking. On the contrary, in my opinion you are very witty—for your age and position.

POLITICIAN.—I was saying, we are now in agreement with the rest of Europe as regards the *cultural* transformation of Turkey, and that we have not, and need not have, any special policy of our own. We must, however, admit that in consequence of our general backwardness, the share of Russia in civilising Turkey has so far not been considerable. Our reputation as a first-class military Power cannot exactly be maintained for the present. Things cannot be got for nothing, they must be earned. We attained our military importance, not by words but by real campaigns and battles. In the same way we must win our cultural importance by labours and victories in peaceful pursuits. If the Turks submitted to our force of arms, they will certainly submit, in the matter of civilisation, to those who are most powerful in the art of culture. What ought we to do? That imaginary Cross on St. Sophia which we raised in opposition to the real, substantial labours of the Germans will scarcely give us the pre-eminence at Constantinople.

GENERAL.—The point is that the Cross should not be imaginary.

POLITICIAN.—Then what is to materialise the Cross? Until you discover such a medium the only thing required to soothe our self-love is to increase our efforts in order to reach the civilisation of more cultured nations instead of wasting our time on Slav committees and other pernicious nonsense. Besides, if it is impossible in Turkey, we can still play an important part in civilising Central Asia and the Far East, whither, it would appear, universal history is transferring its centre of gravity. In consequence of geographical and other conditions, Russia can there achieve more than all the other Powers, with the exception, of course, of England.

The object of our policy in that connection should, therefore, consist in constant and friendly agreements with the English, so that our civilising co-operation with them should never degenerate into senseless quarrels and unworthy rivalry.

Mr. Z.—Unfortunately similar transformations among men as well as in nations are only brought about, as it were, by fate.

Politician.—Yes, that is how it happens. However, neither in the life of men nor of nations do I know a single example where enmity between peoples engaged in the same work made any one stronger, richer or happier. This universal experience is taken into consideration by wise people, and I think that quick-witted Russians will not fail to avail themselves of it ultimately. To quarrel with the English in the Far East would be the height of foolishness, to say nothing of the impropriety of exposing our own differences to strangers. But perhaps we are more nearly related to yellow-faced Chinamen than to the countrymen of Shakespeare and Byron ?

Mr. Z.—That is a delicate matter.

Politician.—Let us put it aside for the present and turn to another question. Will you adopt my point of view and admit that at present the policy of Russia can have only two objects? First, the maintenance of European peace, since every European war in the present state of historical development must be a useless and wicked civil war. And second, the exercise of civilising authority on barbarous nations which are in our sphere of influence.

Both these objects, independently of their intrinsic worth, support and guarantee each other's existence. While working to civilise barbarous countries, which is for the interest of all Europe, we draw more closely the bonds of union between ourselves and other European nations.

The confirmation of European unity, in its turn, strengthens our influence on barbarous nations, depriving them of the thought of opposition. If the yellow race knew that Russia was backed by Europe, our progress in Asia would meet with no obstacles. In the contrary case the yellow race might be inclined to attack our frontier, and we would have to protect ourselves on two fronts, extending to some ten thousand versts. I do not believe in the bogey of Mongolian invasion, because I do not admit the possibility of European war, otherwise we might fear the Mongols.

General.—You consider a European war and an invasion of Mongols improbable, yet I fear that your " solidarity " of the European nations and

WAR AND CHRISTIANITY 77

the advent of universal peace are also improbable. It appears somehow unnatural and improbable. There is good reason for singing in churches on Christmas-day, " Peace on earth and goodwill towards men." That means that there will be peace on earth only when there is goodwill among men. But when will that be ? Have you seen it ? To tell the truth, the only State in Europe that you and I feel friendly towards is the Principality of Monaco. We are always at peace with that State. But close friendship with the Germans and the English and " solidarity " with them, as you call it, will never be realised.

POLITICIAN.—How do you mean it will never be realised; it is already realised, in the natural order of things. We are in " solidarity " with Europeans for the very simple reason that we are Europeans. Since the eighteenth century it has been *un fait accompli*, and neither the barbarity of the masses of the Russian people nor the wild dreams of the Slavophils can change it.

GENERAL.—But is there solidarity among themselves, for instance between Germans, French and English ? We learn that even the Swedes and Norwegians have lost their solidarity.

POLITICIAN.—The argument rests on a false basis, for the historical situation has been lost sight of. Did solidarity exist between Moscow and Novgorod in the time of Ivan III. and Ivan IV. ? Why should you then not admit the existence of the present solidarity of the provinces of Moscow and Novgorod in the general interests of Russia ?

GENERAL.—All I say is, delay proclaiming yourselves Europeans until the European nations form a family, welded together as are the component parts of the Russian Empire. Are we to break up our own solidarity and join the Europeans, who are at daggers drawn among themselves?

POLITICIAN.—At daggers drawn is a strong expression. You may rest in hope. Not only Sweden and Norway, but neither Germany nor France will break up; they will foresee and prevent rupture. The small group of Russian adventurers who back France against Germany ought to be shut up in a fortress, to develop there their patriotism and to preach war against Germany.

LADY.—How fine it would be if all national enmity could be locked up in a fortress! But I think you are mistaken.

POLITICIAN.—Well, of course, I spoke *cum grano salis*. No doubt Europe is not entirely united, but I still maintain my historical analogy.

As it was in Russia in the sixteenth century, so it is now in Europe. Separatism existed, but was then at its last gasp; Imperial unity was no more a dream, but was being moulded into a definite form. National antagonism was still extant, especially among the uneducated masses and politicians, but it lacked the power to act. A European war could not be provoked. As regards the benevolent sentiments to which the General referred, I have seldom seen them among nations or peoples composing a nation, or even in private families. Every one for himself. What deductions are we therefore to make? There is no cause for civil wars and fratricide. It does not matter if Germans and Frenchmen are not partial to each other, provided there is no war. I am convinced that there will be none.

Mr. Z.—That is very probable. But even if we consider Europe as one and indivisible, it in no wise follows that we are Europeans. You know that for more than ten years there has been a notion that the German-Romanic nations have unity in their cultural historical type, but that we Russians form a separate Greco-Slavonic type.

Politician.—I have heard about this variety of Slavophilism and have even conversed with its votaries. What I then noticed enabled me to solve this question. The fact of the matter is that not all those gentlemen who cry out against Europe and our European notions can adhere to the views adopted by our Greco-Slavonic Church. They are invariably carried away by the teaching of Confucius, Buddha, Tibet Lamas and all manner of Indo-Mongolian Orientalism. Their estrangement from Europe is as great as their gravitation towards Asia. What does that mean ? Let us admit that they are right as regards Europe, that it is a great delusion. But why are they so fatally carried away by the other extreme—by this Asiatic propaganda ? And where have their Greco-Slavonic and Orthodox ideas disappeared ? For in them was the pith of the matter. Drive out Nature by the door and it gets in by the window. In this instance Nature has no self-existent Greco-Slavonic, cultural, historical type, but was and is Russia, a great frontier country between Europe and Asia. Being a border land, our country is naturally more influenced by the Asiatic element than other European States. Herein lies the imaginary idea of our Slav self-existence. Even Byzantium has no inherent nationality of its own, but appeared original merely from its Asiatic admixture. In our case, from early days, and especially from the time of Baty, the Asiatic element became a second nature and animated the Russian spirit, so much so that the Germans were able to say about us, although not without a sigh :

"Zwei Seelen wohnen, Ach! in *ihrer* Brust
Die eine will sich von der andern trennen."

To free ourselves from our Oriental spirit is impossible and unnecessary, but we must give the preference to the better and higher spirit, which is more favourable to progress and richer in possibilities. That is what we did under Peter the Great. But our relationship with Asia still gave rise in some minds to chimerical notions advocating the subversion of a great historical question, which had been finally settled. Hence Slavophilism, *i.e.*, a theory of our original, self-existent, historical culture, and so forth. In reality we are unavoidably *Europeans*, only with Asiatic characteristics of mind. This is, so to speak, grammatically self-evident. What is *Russian* in a grammatical sense? It is an adjective; and what substantive does this adjective qualify?

LADY.—I suppose the noun *man :* Russian man, Russian people.

POLITICIAN.—No. It is too broad and indefinite, for even Papuans and Esquimos are men, and have

I, as a man and a noun, anything in common with Papuans and Esquimos ?

LADY.—Nevertheless, some very important things are common to all people ; for instance, love.

POLITICIAN.—That is still wider. How can I admit love as my specific attribute, when I know that it is also natural to all animals and other living creatures ?

MR. Z.—It is a complicated affair. I, for one, am a gentle man, and therefore in love affairs I am more in solidarity with a white or a blue dove than with the Moor, Othello, although he is also called a man.

GENERAL.—Well, at a certain age every reasonable man is in solidarity with the white pigeons.[1]

LADY.—What is that ?

GENERAL.—It is a joke, not for you, but for His Excellency and your humble servant.

POLITICIAN.—Let us drop this. *Trève de plaisanteries.* We are not on the stage of the French theatre. I wished to say that the real substantive for the adjective *Russian* is *European*. We are Russian Europeans just as there are English, French, or German Europeans. If I feel that I am a European, is it not foolish to try and prove that I am a kind of Slavo-Russ or Greco-Slav ? I know that I am a European as surely as I am a Russian. I can, and perhaps I ought, to be kind and compassionate towards every man as well as to every animal, because blessed is the man who is merciful to his beast. I cannot, however, consider myself in solidarity or close friendship with Zulus or China-

[1] A certain Russian sect.

men, but only with nations and peoples who have
created and preserved the treasures of higher
culture, which contribute to my spiritual nourish-
ment and afford me supreme happiness. Originally
war was a sacred duty enabling chosen nations to
be formed and consolidated in order to withstand the
lower elements of humanity. Now they have been
formed and consolidated, and they have nothing to
fear except internecine quarrels. The epoch of
peace and the spread of peaceful European culture
is now everywhere on the increase. All must become
Europeans. The ideal European should be the ideal
of all humanity, and European culture, the aim of
all mankind. In this lies the meaning of history.
At first there were only Greek and Roman Europeans.
Next appeared others, some in the West, some in the
East. There were also Russian Europeans. On
the other side of the ocean appeared American
Europeans, and now we must expect Turkish,
Persian, Indian, Japanese, and perhaps Chinese
Europeans. A European is at present a definite
mental conception which is extending in every sense.
Observe, however, the difference. Every man is
like any other man. Therefore, if we accept this
abstract idea as our essential, we must admit entire
personal equality and value the nation of Newton
and Shakespeare no higher than we value a nation
of Papuans. But this is ridiculous and, in practice,
objectionable. If my mental conception is not a
man in general, but one who spreads culture—*i.e.*,
a European—then the idea of equality is nonsense.
The idea conveyed by the term *European* is the same

as the idea conveyed by the word *culture*, which is a sound standard or measurement for the definition of comparative worth or value of different races, nations and individuals. These different evaluations must be taken into consideration by sound politicians. Otherwise, if we place comparatively cultured Austrians on the same platform with semi-barbarous Herzegovinians, we shall come to the same foolish and dangerous speculations which attract the latest Mohicans of our Slavophilism. *Il y a Européen et Européen*. Even after the advent of that desirable and, I trust, not far distant hour, when Europe, or the cultured world, will really embrace all the inhabitants of the terrestrial globe in a united and peaceful humanity, there will still remain those natural gradations and shades of culture, canonised by history, which are to determine our relations with different nationalities. In the glorious, all-comprising kingdom of higher culture, just as in the kingdom of heaven, there is one glory of the sun, another glory of the moon, another glory of the stars, one star differeth from another; such is, I believe, the teaching of our catechism. And now, although the goal is near, but not attained, it is all the more necessary to beware of the error of indiscriminate equality. At present the newspapers have been writing about the quarrel between England and the Transvaal, and that the Africanders even threaten England with war. And I foresee that some of our journalists and politicians, and perhaps some on the Continent, will take the side of these, so-called, down-trodden Africanders.

Why, it would be as if our highly-respected Mr. Maartens[1] were to go into a grocer's shop and be attacked and ill-treated by a vulgar clerk on the plea that the shop was his and not Mr. Maartens'. One might regret that Mr. Maartens got into this dilemma, but when he was once in it I, for one, would be gratified if Mr. Maartens had the clerk taken up by the police and relegated to a house of correction. But, instead of that, various decently-attired gentlemen commend the grocer's boy. "Such a small chap, and had the pluck to attack a tall, fine gentleman." If the Africander traders and carriers had the sense to declare themselves Dutchmen—their blood relations, they might consider themselves a special nationality calculated to found their own African fatherland. Oh, the rascal!

LADY.—In the first place, don't be abusive; and secondly, explain to me what is this Transvaal. What kind of people are the inhabitants?

MR. Z.—The inhabitants are a mixture of Europeans and niggers. They are neither white nor black, but they are Boers.

LADY.—I presume that is also a joke.

POLITICIAN.—And a poor one.

MR. Z.—The jokes are as good as the Boers. Besides, if you object to the colour, they have also an *Orange* State.

POLITICIAN.—Speaking seriously, I may say that these Boers are certainly Europeans, but poor specimens. Separated from their glorious metro-

---

[1] The late eminent Russian jurisconsult of International Law.

polis, they have lost to a great extent their culture ; surrounded by natives, they have become uncivilised. To place them on a par with the English, and wish them to be successful in the struggle with England— *cela n'a pas de nom.*

LADY.—But our Europeans sympathised with the Circassian mountaineers when they fought with us for their independence, and Russia is more cultured than the Circassians.

POLITICIAN.—In order not to expatiate on the causes of this European sympathy with the Circassian barbarians, I will merely observe that we should assimilate the general tendency of European thought, and not the occasional foolishness of some Europeans. I regret with all my heart that England may have to resort to such superannuated and objectionable means as war, to pacify the pugnacious people who have challenged her. Should war, however, be unavoidable in consequence of the savagery of these Zulus—I meant to say Boers— encouraged by the jealousy of the Continent against England, I should, of course, sincerely wish that this war might end with the complete pacification of the African roughs, so that their independence should be destroyed once for all. On the other hand their success, which is not impossible as Africa is far away, would be the triumph of barbarity over civilisation, and for me, as a Russian, *i.e.*, a European, it would be a day of deep national mourning.

MR. Z. (*sotto voce*).—The statesman speaks eloquently, like that Frenchman : *ce sabre d'honneur est le plus beau jour de ma vie.*

Lady (*to the Politician*).—No, I don't agree. And why not sympathise with these Boers ? Did not we sympathise with William Tell ?

Politician.—Yes, if they had created their own poetical legend, inspired a home-bred Jean Jacques Rousseau and produced authors and scientists, we would speak differently of them.

Lady.—But all this civilisation might come later. To begin with, the Swiss were likewise shepherds. . . . And the Americans, when they fought for their independence against the English, were not bereft of civilisation. Although not Boers, they tore off the scalps of the Red Indians, as Mayne Reid tells us. Lafayette also sympathised with them, and he was right, because they have now joined all religions together and made an exhibition of them at Chicago, a thing which had never been done before. In Paris the French wanted to do the same thing, but nothing came of it. An *abbé*, called Victor Charbonnel, was also very active about it. He wrote to me several times : a very sympathetic man. But the various religions could not agree. Even the Chief Rabbi declared that " for religion we have the Bible, and an exhibition was out of place." Poor Charbonnel was in such despair that he abjured Christ and announced in the newspapers that he had resigned his living and greatly respected Renan. The end of his career, I am told, was not satisfactory, for he married, or took to drink or did something of the kind. Next came our Nepluef, who finally lost faith in all religions. He wrote to me that he only believed in humanity. He is an idealist. But how was humanity to be represented at the Paris Exhibition? I think it is all too fantastic. The Americans have, however, arranged matters very cleverly. Ecclesiastics representing all religions joined them. A Catholic bishop was elected president. He read out the Lord's Prayer in English, while the Buddhist and Chinese idolatrous priests responded very politely: "Oh yes! All right, sir!"[1] We wish no one evil, and we only beg one thing, that your missionaries should keep away from us. Your religion is very good for you, but you do not practise it. That is not our fault, but our religions are the best for us." And so everything finished satisfactorily, there was no fighting, but much astonishment. Who knows, perhaps these Africanders may become Americans.

POLITICIAN.—Certainly, all things are possible. Even a *garroche* may become an eminent man of science. But in the meantime, for his own good it might be as well to give him a flogging.

LADY.—What language! *Décidément vous vous encanaillez?* All this comes from Monte Carlo. *Qui est-ce que vous fréquentez là bas? Les familles des croupiers, sans doute?* However, that is your business. I would only beg you to curtail your political wisdom or we shall be late for dinner. It is time to stop.

POLITICIAN.—My wish was to sum up, to wind up and to connect the end with the beginning.

LADY.—You will never finish. I must assist to

[1] "Oh yes! All right, sir!" in English in the original text.—ED.

explain your idea. You meant to say, formerly there was a God and there was war, and that now instead of God we have culture and peace. Is that so?

POLITICIAN.—Perhaps. Thereabouts.

LADY.—That's all right. What is God? Although I do not know and cannot explain, I feel He exists. But as regards your culture, I feel nothing. Explain to me in two words what it is.

POLITICIAN.—Of what culture consists and what it contains, you know yourself. It is all the treasures of thought and genius which have been created by the greatest minds of chosen nations.

LADY.—That is not one thing, but several different things. Here is Voltaire, Bossuet, also the Madonna and Nana, and Alfred Musset and Philaret. Are they to form one mass, and that mass to replace God?

POLITICIAN.—Yes, I meant to say that we need not trouble about culture in the sense of an historical depositary of treasures. It is created; it exists, and we thank God for it. We might hope that there will be new Shakespeares and Newtons, but that is not in our power and is of no practical interest. There is, however, another practical or moral side to culture. In private life we call it politeness or courteousness. This may appear unimportant to a superficial observer, but it has an immense and exclusive meaning, because it may be universal and obligatory. One cannot demand exalted virtues or genius, but one can and must insist on politeness from everybody. It is that *minimum* of consideration for others and of morality, thanks to which people can live together as human beings. Certainly, politeness is not the *whole* of culture, just as reading and writing does not exhaust mental development, but politeness is one of its conditions. Politeness is culture *à l'usage de tout le monde*. And we see that from private relations it extends to all social classes, political and international. We remember how in our childhood people could be rude and unrefined, but now obligatory and even coercive politeness has extended its power, and is reaching all classes and countries.

LADY.—Pray be brief. You are trying to prove that peaceful politics between States is the same thing as politeness between people.

POLITICIAN.—Certainly. In French, *politesse* and *politique* are closely connected. And observe, that no sentiments or special benevolence are required in this case, as the gallant General needlessly observed. If I do not assault a person, it does not follow that I am benevolently inclined towards him. On the contrary, I may harbour hostile sentiments in my heart, but as a cultured man I scorn quarrels. I also realise that no good can come of fighting. I therefore treat the man with politeness, thereby losing nothing and gaining much. Just in the same way, whatever antipathy may exist between two more or less civilised nations, they will never resort to *des voies de fait*—*i.e.*, to war, for the two following reasons. Firstly, because war is not as represented in poetry and in pictures, but as it exists in reality. Dead bodies, festering wounds, a collection of coarse and dirty people, the interruption of the natural course of life, the destruction of useful edifices and institutions, of bridges, railroads, telegraphs—all this dismal medley is revolting to a cultured nation just as mangled bodies disgust us. Secondly, a nation which has attained a certain degree of intellectual development comprehends how advantageous it is to be polite towards other nations, and how unprofitable it is to fight with them. There are certainly various gradations: hitting with the fist is more cultured than biting, caning is more cultured than hitting, and a symbolic slap on the face is still more civilised. Wars can also be waged in a more or less barbarous manner, and the European wars of the nineteenth century are more like old-fashioned duels between respectable men than a stand-up fight between two drunken apprentices. But even this is a passing phase. You may have observed that among advanced nations even duels are going out of fashion. While backward Russia is deploring the death of her best poets killed in duels, in more civilised France duels have become bloodless combats, the remnants of a bad and *defunct* tradition. "*Quand on est mort c'est qu'on n'est plus en vie*," said de la Palisse, famous for his truisms. And believe me that you and I will see duels and wars buried in the archives of history. Real culture requires that all *fighting* between men as well as nations should be abolished. In every case a peaceful policy is the best criterion and evidence of progress in civilisation. And, therefore, with every desire to be agreeable to our gallant General, I still maintain my statement that literary agitation against war is of good augur. It not only prevents, but it also hastens the final solution of the problem. With all its strange enthusiasm, this propaganda is important because it emphasises to the public mind the great fact of historical progress. A peaceful, *i.e.*, polite, all-round profitable adjustment of all international relations and differences is the stable form of sound politics for civilised humanity. (*Turning to Mr. Z.*) You wish to say something.

MR. Z.—You lately said that a peaceful policy is a symptom of progress. In that connection I remember that in Turgenyef's "Smoke" somebody very justly observed: "Progress is a symptom." In that case would it not follow that peaceful policy is a symptom of a symptom?

POLITICIAN.—Yes. And what then? Certainly everything is relative. But what is your idea?

MR. Z.—Merely this, that if peaceful politics are only the shadow of a shadow, is it worth talking so much about all this shadowy progress? Would it not be preferable to tell humanity what Father Varsonovius said to the religious lady: "You are old and weak, and will never be any better."

LADY.—Now this comes too late. (*To the Politician.*) Observe how your own *politique-politesse* mocks you.

POLITICIAN.—How is that?

LADY.—Only that you will not go to-morrow to Monte Carlo, *euphemistically* called Nice.

POLITICIAN.—Why so?

LADY.—Because these gentlemen wish to refute you, but you were so prolix that no time is left for them, and their arguments will have to be put off till to-morrow. But is it possible that while *cultured* people will be contradicting your theses you will be at Monte Carlo enjoying more or less forbidden pleasures with uneducated croupiers and their families? That would be the height of rudeness. Where, then, is your " obligatory minimum " of virtue?

POLITICIAN.—If such is the case, I can put off my trip to Nice for a day or two, as I am curious to hear what can be said against my axioms.

LADY.—That's right. And now I think we are all very hungry. If it had not been for our *culture* some of us would have escaped long ago to the dining-room.

POLITICIAN.—It appears to me that culture and the culinary art are closely united.

LADY.—Oh, dear, another joke!

And thereupon, after exchanging some doubtful witticisms, all followed the lady to her hospitable board.

THE THIRD CONVERSATION

"*Audiatur et* tertia *pars*."

ON this occasion, by mutual consent, we assembled in the garden earlier than usual, so as not to be hurried at the end of the conversation. Consequently all were in a more serious frame of mind than the evening before.

POLITICIAN (*to Mr. Z.*).—You, I believe, wished to raise an objection to something or to make a remark upon what I said recently?

MR. Z.—Yes; with reference to your definition that a peace policy is a symptom of progress, I remembered at once the words of one of the characters in Turgenyef's "Smoke" that "progress is a symptom." I do not know precisely what Turgenyef's character meant by this, but surely the natural meaning of those words is quite accurate. Progress is, in fact, a symptom.

POLITICIAN.—Of what?

MR. Z.—It is a pleasure to be talking with intelligent people. It was exactly to this question that I was leading the conversation. I consider that progress—that is, visible, rapid progress—is always *a symptom of the end*.

POLITICIAN.—I understand that where there is such progress as, for example, in a case of creeping paralysis, that is a symptom of the end. But in the case of culture or civilisation, why must progress infallibly be a symptom of the end?

MR. Z.—Well, it is not so apparent as in the case of paralysis; nevertheless, it is so.

POLITICIAN.—You are convinced, that is clear enough; but to me it is not even clear what it is of which you are convinced. In the first place, I am encouraged by your praise to put again the simple question, which you thought clever. You say, "a symptom of the end." The end of *what?* I ask.

MR. Z.—The end of that of which we were talking. We were discussing the history of mankind; that historic "process" which certainly has begun to go at an accelerated speed, and as I am convinced draws near to its conclusion.

LADY.—*C'est la fin du monde, n'est ce pas?* This is very curious.

GENERAL.—Well, at last we have reached the most interesting point.

PRINCE.—I suppose, though, you will not be able to leave out "Antichrist"?

MR. Z.—Certainly not, it has the first place.

PRINCE (*to the Lady*).—Please excuse me, I have a terrible amount of very pressing business, so that with every wish to listen to such interesting things, I must go home.

GENERAL.—What? Then how about vint?

POLITICIAN.—I had a presentiment the day before yesterday that there would be some unpleasantness. When once religion comes in, expect trouble.

"Tantum religio potuit suadere malorum."

PRINCE.—There will be no unpleasantness. I shall endeavour to return at nine o'clock, but now I really have no time.

LADY.—But why such haste? Why did you not think about those important matters before? I do not believe you. You must admit that it is " Antichrist " that has suddenly frightened you away.

PRINCE.—I heard so much yesterday about politeness being the thing of first importance that, acting under that suggestion, I decided to tell an untruth for the sake of politeness. Now, I see, that this is very wrong, and I will say frankly that, though I have in fact important business, I am leaving this conversation chiefly because I consider it useless to waste my time in an argument about things such as may have some meaning, possibly, for papooses.

POLITICIAN.—Evidently you have now expiated your serious sin of excessive politeness.

LADY.—Why get angry? If we are stupid, enlighten us. Look at me, I certainly am not angry because you called me a papoose. Even papooses may have true understanding. God reveals his wisdom to babes. But if you find it hard to listen to conversation about Antichrist, very well, we will make peace about that. Your villa is only a step or two from here. Go away now, attend to your business, but come back for the end of the conversation, after Antichrist.

PRINCE.—Very well, I will come back.

(*When the Prince had gone the* GENERAL *remarked, laughing*).—The cat knows whose meat she has eaten.

LADY.—What! Do you think, for instance, that our Prince is Antichrist?

GENERAL.—No, not personally; not he personally: it's a long way from the caterpillar to the butterfly! All the same, he is in that line. As St. John the Divine has already said in his epistle: "You have heard, little children, that Antichrist shall come; even now are there many Antichrists." So, you see, among those many; among the many, I say . . .

LADY.—You may, perchance, find yourself among the "many." On him God will not be hard; they have led him astray. He knows that he will never do anything remarkable, only walk about in a smart uniform and set himself up as though he had got into the guards from a line regiment. To a great general all this does not matter, but it turns the head of a little officer.

POLITICIAN.—That is good psychology. All the same, I do not understand why he became angry at the mention of Antichrist. Here am I, for instance. I do not believe in anything mystic, yet it does not make me angry, but rather interests me from the human point of view. I know that to many it is a serious matter; that is to say, it gives expression to a certain side of human nature which is somewhat atrophied in me, but it preserves its objective interest for me too. For example, I am altogether bad at painting and can draw nothing—not even a straight line or a circle—so I do not discuss amongst painters what is well drawn and what badly drawn. But I am interested in questions of painting on educational and æsthetic grounds.

LADY.—On such an inoffensive subject as that one cannot get angry ; but you yourself hate religion, and just now quoted some Latin abuse against it.

POLITICIAN.—Well, was it abuse ? I, like my favourite poet Lucretius, blame religion for bloody altars and for the wailing of human victims. The echo of this bloodthirstiness I hear in the gloomy, intolerant statements of our friend who has just left the discussion. But religious ideas in themselves interest me very much, and, among others, this idea of "Antichrist." Unfortunately, on this subject I happen to have read only a book of Renan, and he treats the matter merely on the side of historical learning, and applies everything to Nero. But that is nothing. Of course the idea of Antichrist existed much earlier amongst the Hebrews than in the time of Nero, arising out of King Antiochus Epiphanes, and it has lasted on from that time, for example, among our schismatics. It is a kind of general idea.

GENERAL.—Yes, it is all very well for your Excellency to reflect on such things in your leisure moments, but our poor Prince is so engrossed in Evangelical propaganda that he is never able to deliberate about Christ or Antichrist ; he has not even got more than three hours in the day left for playing vint. He is an honest man, and one must give him his due.

LADY.—No, you are too hard on him. Of course all such people are confused, but we must remember that they are also unhappy, for there is no joy, ease, or peace in their lives. And, you know, somewhere in the Scriptures it is said that Christianity is joy in the Holy Ghost.

GENERAL.—The position is indeed oppressive ; not having the spirit of Christ and yet pretending to be true Christians.

MR. Z.—*Particularly* for Christians, not having the very thing which is the particular feature of Christianity.

GENERAL.—But it seems to me that this sad position is the precise position of Antichrist which for the more wise or enlightened is overburdened with the consciousness that in the long run deceit, of course, will not pay.

MR. Z.—At all events, it is certain that the idea of Antichrist, which according to its Biblical interpretation—both of the Old and New Testaments—is the last act of the historic tragedy, will not be simple unbelief or negation of Christianity, or materialism and such like, but that it will be religious *imposture*, when with the name of Christ will be associated forces in human nature which are in fact and in essence foreign, and plainly hostile to Christ and His Spirit.

GENERAL.—Well, of course the devil would not be the devil if he were to play in the open !

POLITICIAN.—I fear, then, lest all Christians should turn out to be impostors and therefore according to you, Antichrists. The only possible exceptions would be the unconscious masses of the people, as far as such still exist in the Christian world, together with a certain number of individual cranks, like you, Sir. But in any case, one ought to regard as Antichrists those people—both here in France and with us—who particularly make a fuss about Christianity, who make of it their special occupation, and make it the profession of a sort of monopoly or privilege of their own. Such people at the present time belong to one of two classes which are equally foreign, I hope, to the spirit of Christ. Either some sort of murderous shearers, who are ready at once to restore the Inquisition and to arrange religious massacres, like those pious abbots and "brave" "Catholic" officers who not long ago expressed their best sentiments on the occasion of the festival of a certain depraved[1] rascal; or that of the novel fasters and celibates who discovered virtue and conscience as a kind of America, and in other respects have lost interior truthfulness and all common sense. The first sort causes moral nausea and the second sort induces physical yawning.

GENERAL.—Yes, in former times Christianity was incomprehensible to some and odious to others; but it is only now that it has become repulsive. I can imagine how the devil rubbed his hands and hugged himself at such a success. Gracious heavens!

[1] Evidently POLITICIAN alludes to the document drawn up in memory of the suicide Henri, wherein one French officer stated that he signed in the hope of a new St. Bartholomew's Day, another that he hoped for a speedy hanging of all Protestants, Freemasons, and Jews, and a certain abbot that he lived in the hope of that bright future, when the skins of flayed Huguenots, Masons, and Jews would be made into cheap carpets, and he as a good Christian would constantly trample upon such a carpet with his feet. These statements out of some tens of thousands of others of the same kind were printed in the newspaper *Libre Parole*.

Lady.—So that is Antichrist in your opinion?

Mr. Z.—Well, no; I have only given some explanatory suggestions about its nature: the real thing is still to come.

Lady.—Is that the simplest explanation you can give of what the thing is?

Mr. Z.—Well, I cannot guarantee simplicity. You do not light upon true simplicity all at once, and so-called simplicity is artificial, false—nothing is worse than that. There is an old proverb which a friend of mine, now dead, loved to repeat; great simplicity is easily misleading.

Lady.—Well, that itself is not altogether simple.

General.—It is apparently the same as the popular proverb; some simplicity is worse than robbery.

Mr. Z.—It is the same.

Lady.—Now even I can understand.

Mr. Z.—I am only sorry that you don't give your whole explanation of Antichrist in proverbs.

Lady.—Well, explain it as you know it.

Mr. Z.—First of all, tell me, do you grant the existence and power of evil in the world?

Lady.—I would rather not grant it, but there it is inevitably. What do you make of death, for one thing? Anyhow, you can't escape that evil. I believe that "the last enemy to be destroyed is death"; now so long as it is not destroyed, it is evident that evil is not only strong, but is stronger than good.

Mr. Z. (*to the General*).—And what do you think?

General.—I never shut my eyes in face of bullets

and shot, so I shall not begin to flinch at more slender questions. Certainly evil exists just as really as good. God exists and the devil also exists —of course, only so long as God allows him.

POLITICIAN.—For myself I answer nothing. My opinion does not go to the root of things, but I explained yesterday as well as I could, that side of the matter which is clear to me. But I am anxious to become acquainted with other views. The Prince's line of thought is well known to me, that is to say, I know that for me there is no actual meaning in it at all, only a mere pretence, *qui n'a rime ni raison*. But the positive religious view is, of course, more persistent and interests me more. Hitherto I have only been acquainted with it in its official form, which does not satisfy me. I should very much like to hear, at last, not beautiful phrases about these things, but a natural human account of them.

MR. Z.—Of all the stars which rise in the intellectual horizon of a man who reads attentively our sacred books, there is none in my opinion more brilliant and astonishing than that which shines in the phrase of the Gospel, " Suppose ye that I am come to give peace on earth ? I tell you, Nay ; but rather divisions." He came to bring *truth* on earth, but *truth*, like good, before all else *divides*.

LADY.—This needs explanation. Why did Christ call Himself *prince de la paix*, and why did He also say that peacemakers are called sons of God ?

MR. Z.—And are you really wishing me to obtain that higher status by reconciling contradictory texts ?

Lady.—Precisely.

Mr. Z.—Well, notice that the only way of reconciling them is by making a distinction between good or true peace and the peace which is bad or false. This distinction is plainly pointed out by Him who brought a true peace and a good enmity : " Peace I leave with you, My peace I give unto you : not as the world giveth, give I unto you." That is to say, there is the good peace of Christ founded on this division that Christ came to bring on earth, namely, on the distinction between good and evil, between truth and falsehood ; and there is the bad peace of the world, founded on a confusion or merely exterior unity of that which inwardly is at enmity with itself.

Lady.—How do you explain the difference between good and bad peace ?

Mr. Z.—Almost in the same way as the General did three days ago, when he jokingly observed that there is such a thing as a good peace, for example, the peace of Nishstadt or of Kutchuk-Kainardzh. Underlying this joke there is a more general and important idea. In spiritual strife as in political, a good peace is one which is concluded only on obtaining the object of the war.

Lady.—But in the last resort whence arises the war between good and evil ? Is it absolutely necessary for them to fight one against the other ? And can there be between them a real collision—*corps à corps ?* Of course in an ordinary war, when one side begins to be reinforced and then the other opposing side seeks reinforcements, the quarrel must be settled by actual battles, with guns and bayonets. But in the struggle between good and evil this is not so, and when the good side is reinforced, the bad side at once becomes enfeebled and it never comes to an actual pitting of one against the other, so that all this is only in a figurative sense. That is, it is only necessary to make sure that the good in people is the greater, then the evil at once will be the less.

Mr. Z.—That is, you think that if only good people themselves would become still better, then the bad people would lose their badness till finally they also become good?

Lady.—It seems to me that is so.

Mr. Z.—Well, are any occasions known to you when the goodness of a good man made the bad man good or at least less evil?

Lady.—No; to tell the truth, I have neither seen such occasions nor heard—but stop, what you said just now corresponds, I think, with the subject of your conversation with the Prince the day before yesterday concerning the fact that even Christ with all His goodness could do no good to the soul of Judas Iscariot or the wicked thief. As the answer to this was left for the Prince, do not forget about it when he comes.

Mr. Z.—Well, since I do not take him for Antichrist, I do not believe in his coming, still less in his theological readiness. But not wishing that this undecided question should clog our conversation, I offer meanwhile this answer, which the Prince ought to work out from *his own point of view*, " Why did not Christ in His goodness regenerate the evil souls of Judas and Co. ? " Simply because men were then too much in the dark and only very few souls had reached the stage of moral development in which the inward strength of truth can be perceptible. Judas and Co. were still too " undeveloped." Now Christ Himself said to His disciples : " The works that I do, shall ye do also—and greater than these shall ye do "; which means that, in the higher degree of moral progress to which mankind has attained in our days, the true disciples of Christ are able, in the strength of their gentleness and non-resistance to evil, to do moral wonders greater than those which were possible eighteen centuries ago. . . .

GENERAL.—Excuse me ! If they *are able* to do so why don't they do so ? Have you seen these new wonders ? Why, look at our Prince, even now, " after eighteen centuries of the moral development of the Christian conscience," he is in no way able to enlighten my dark soul ; I remain the same savage that I was before I met him, and still, as formerly, after God and Russia, I love most of all in the world the work of the army in general and of the artillery in particular. And, moreover, our Prince is not the only one I have encountered, I have met many other non-resisters mightier than he.

MR. Z.—Now, why get on to such personal grounds ? and what do you want of me ? I put before you on behalf of our absent opponent a passage of the Gospel which he had forgotten, and beyond that

> " Whether it reason or unreason seem—
> I do not answer for another's dream."

LADY.—Henceforward I too shall take the part of the poor Prince. If he wished to be wise he would answer the General thus: " I and others like me, whom you have met, count ourselves true disciples of Christ only in regard to our thoughts and conduct, not on the grounds that we have greater powers. But, in fact, there do exist somewhere, or soon will, Christians more perfect than we are— they may penetrate your stronghold of darkness."

MR. Z.—This answer, of course, would be of practical utility were it not that it made its appeal to unknown instances. But as it is, it is not serious. They, let us suppose, say, indeed they must say—we can do nothing either greater than that which Christ did, nor equal to His works nor even less than them, but only something which approximates to them. What in sound logic must be deduced from such an avowal?

GENERAL.—Apparently, only this, that the words of Christ: " Ye shall do what I have done and greater works than these " were said not to these men, but to some other person altogether unlike them.

LADY.—Still, one can imagine that some man might observe to the end the commandment of Christ about love towards enemies and forgiveness of injuries, and that then he would receive through that same Christ, the power to convert by his gentleness evil souls into good ones.

MR. Z.—An experiment of this kind was made not so long ago; not only did it fail, but it proved the direct opposite of what you propound. There was a man who knew no limits to his gentleness, and who not only forgave every injury, but met every new injury with new and increasing acts of kindness. Well, what happened? Did he awaken the soul of his enemy; did he regenerate him morally? Alas! he only hardened the heart of the evil-doer, and fell by his hand in a piteous manner.

LADY.—What are you talking about? Who is this man? Where and when did he live?

MR. Z.—Not so long ago, and in Petersburg. I thought you knew him. He was the chamberlain Delario.

LADY.—I have never heard of him, and I thought I could tell off the whole of Petersburg on my fingers.

POLITICIAN.—I, also, do not remember him. But what is the history of this chamberlain?

MR. Z.—It is excellently set forth in an unpublished poem of Alexis Tolstoy.

LADY.—Unpublished? Then, of course, it is a mere farce. What has this got to do with serious matters?

MR. Z.—I assure you that, though a farce in form, yet it has a real content which is very serious and essentially true. At any rate, the actual relation between good and evil in human life is expressed in these playful verses far better than I could explain it with my serious prose. Of one thing I have not the least doubt. When the heroes of some world-renowned novels, in which the black soil of psychology is skilfully and seriously ploughed up, become mere literary reminiscences for bookmen, this farce will retain all its artistic and philosophical truth, because, though proceeding on comic and wildly caricaturing lines, it has touched the subsoil depth of the moral question.

LADY.—Well, I do not believe in your paradoxes. You are afflicted with the spirit of contradiction, and you always defy public opinion on purpose.

MR. Z.—I should probably defy it if it existed. But all the same, I will tell you the story of the chamberlain Delario as you do not know it, and I remember it by heart.

> The wicked robber plunged his dagger
>   In the breast of Delario ;
> And he, for his part, lifted his hat and said,
>   " Dear Sir, I thank you."
> Then in the left side the robber struck again
>   His dreadful dagger,
> And Delario said, " What a splendid dagger
>   That is of yours."
> Then also the right side this cruel robber
>   Pierced as before,
> But Delario with a gentle smile
>   Barely reproved him.
> The miscreant then raised his dagger up
>   And struck him in a hundred places ;
> Said Delario, " I pray you, Sir,
>   To come to tea at three o'clock to-morrow."
> The wicked man in tears then fell upon the ground
>   And trembled like a leaf.
> But Delario said, " Oh, oh, dear Sir, get up,
>   The floor is dirty " ;
> But the robber would not be comforted
>   And wept the more.
> Then Delario said, " How strange is this !
>   I could not have expected it ;
> To weep in such a way for such a little thing
>   Isn't possible !

I'll let you have a nice estate to farm,
    The order of Stanislas
I'll pin upon your breast, friend,
    For an example.
A word from me to the authorities procures it—
    I'm chamberlain.
My daughter Dunia in marriage
    I will give,
And a hundred thousand roubles, Sir,
    My daughter's dowry.
Meanwhile do take this little portrait of myself
    In memory.
I'm sorry it is not framed, but take it so
    From me."
The murderer got up, but bitterer than pepper
    Was his mood ;
The portrait gift he could forgive,
    But not the offers.
He hardly had the Stanlislavsky order
    Upon his breast
Than a godless rage possessed him, and his dagger
    Dipped he in poison,
And he laid in wait for Delario
    And stabbed him once again.
Down fell Delario to the ground, being unable
    To remain in his armchair,
And the other rushed upstairs and in the *entresol*
    Seduced his daughter,
And then fled to Tambof, where, as Governor,
    He was by all beloved.
Afterward he lived in Moscow, a senator
    By all esteemed.
Then our House of Lords he joined
    For a short season.
What an example was he to us all,
    And what a lesson !

LADY.—How charming, and I did not expect it.

POLITICIAN.—Really excellent. "My daughter's dowry"—admirable. "Not the offers!" and "Then fled to Tambof!"—*deux vrais coups de maitre!*

MR. Z.—But what uprightness, you notice. Delario was not that polished benefactor who is never met with in real life. He was a living man with all the human failings—both boastful (I am a chamberlain) and covetous (a hundred thousand laid by)—and his fantastic impenetrability to the assassin's dagger is only a sign of his boundless good nature, invincible and almost insensible to all affronts, such as does exist, though very rarely. Delario is not the personification of virtue, but a naturally good man whose goodness of heart has overcome the bad qualities and thrust them out on to the soul's surface in the form of inoffensive weaknesses. Likewise, the villain is in no sense merely a walking extract of vice, but an ordinary mixture of good and bad qualities ; but in him the evil of envy was seated in the lowest depths of his soul and thrust out all good on to the *epidermis* of the soul, so to speak, where goodness took the form of a very living but superficial sensitiveness. When to a list of cruel injuries Delario answered with polite words and an invitation to a cup of tea, the sensitiveness of the "villain's" moral epidermis was strongly touched by these manifestations of good feeling, and he gave himself up to the most expansive regret. When also the politeness of the chamberlain passed into the heartfelt sympathy of a truly good man, who repays his foe for evil not only by showing the goodness of polite words and actions, but by real and living goodness of practical aid—when Delario entered into the condition of life of his villain, ready to share with him his means, make arrangements for his official affairs and even his domestic happiness—then this *real* goodness, penetrating the deepest moral stratum of the villain, discloses his interior moral worthlessness, and reaching at length the bottom of his soul, rouses up there a crocodile of envy. The villain is not envious of the goodness of Delario; he himself, of course, might be good, only he did not feel his goodness when he "wept in heartfelt pain." No, he is, in fact, envious of the unfathomable depth and *absolute seriousness* of this goodness. Is not this real; does it not happen in real life? From one and the same moisture of fertilising rain there spring both the beneficial forces of wholesome herbs and the poison of the poisonous. Likewise also a real good deed in the last resort increases the good in the good and the evil in the evil. Ought we, then—have we the right—to give free scope, always and without discrimination, to our good feelings? Ought we to praise parents who zealously water poisonous herbs with a good watering-can in a garden where their children are walking? What about the betrayal of Dunia, I ask you?

GENERAL.—That is evident! If only Delario had moderately hit his villain on the head and driven him out of the house, then, of course, he would not have got so far as the *entresol*.

MR. Z.—In fact, allow him to have the right to sacrifice himself to his goodness; allow that, as in times of yore, there were martyrs of the faith, so now there must be martyrs of goodness. But about Dunia; what is to be done, I ask you? You see, she is simple and young, and to argue anything for herself she is neither able nor willing. So must we not be sorry for her?

POLITICIAN.—I agree we must be sorry. But I, myself, am still more sorry that Antichrist, apparently, has run away from us together with the villain to Tambof.

MR. Z.—We will catch him, your Excellency; we will catch him! Yesterday you were pleased to interpret history as meaning that primitive mankind —consisting originally of a multitude of more or less savage peoples, different from each other, in part unknown to one another and, in part, at enmity with one another—by degrees evolves out of itself the best educated part, the civilised or European world, which gradually increases and spreads, and finally must embrace all the peoples that are left behind in this historic movement, including them all in one solid and peaceful international unity. The establishment of a lasting international peace— that is your formula, is it not?

POLITICIAN.—Yes, and that formula, when it attains to the realisation which awaits it even in the near future, will accomplish many more substantial triumphs of civilisation than can now appear. Only reflect how much bad will of necessity be atrophied, and how much good, in the very nature of things, will break forth and unfold, how much force will be set free for productive occupations, how science and the arts will flourish, and trade, and commerce . . .

Mr. Z.—Well, but the abolition of disease and death, do you include that in the number of the future triumphs of civilisation?

Politician.—Of course, to some extent. Now, already, much has been done in the direction of sanitation, hygiene, antiseptics, organotherapeutics . . .

Mr. Z.—But do these undoubted triumphs on the positive side really balance the undoubted increase of the symptoms of degeneracy in the spheres of neuropathology and psychopathology, symptoms which accompany the advance of civilisation?

Politician.—Well, in what sort of scales is that to be weighed?

Mr. Z.—At any rate, it is incontestable that the plus increases and the minus increases, and the result is something not far from nought. That is the balance-sheet as regards diseases. Now with reference to death, the advance of civilisation, apparently, is represented simply by nought.

Politician.—Indeed, does the advance of civilisation set itself such a problem as the abolition of death?

Mr. Z.—I know that it does not set this, but, of course, for that very reason it cannot itself be set very high. Now, in fact, if I knew for certain that both I myself and all that is dear to me must for ever disappear, would it not be all the same to me whether various people, somewhere or other, were fighting amongst themselves or living in peace, whether they were civilised or savage, polite or impolite?

POLITICIAN.—Yes, from a personal, egoistical point of view, certainly it would be all the same.

MR. Z.—From an egoistical? Excuse me, from every point of view. Death equalises all, and in face of it egoism and altruism, in like manner, are foolish.

POLITICIAN.—Be it so, but you know the foolishness of egoism does not prevent us from being egoists, and in the same way altruism (as far as it is in general possible) is really achieved without any reasonable motives, and the question of death has no significance. I know that my children and grandchildren will die, but this does not hinder me from looking after their welfare as if it were eternal. I labour for them chiefly because I love them, and to give my life up to them gives me satisfaction. "I find a certain gusto in it." *C'est simple comme bonjour.*

LADY.—Yes, so long as all goes well—though even then the thought of death comes in all the same. Now, how about the time when various misfortunes begin with the children and grandchildren? What satisfaction and what gusto then? It is just like the water-lily in the swamp—you grasp, and fall in.

MR. Z.—Yes, and besides this, in the case of children and grandchildren, it is of the very nature of things that you take care of them *quand même*, not waiting to solve or even consider the question as to whether your care can afford them real and final good. You take trouble about them not for some end, but *because* you have a living affection for them; but it is impossible to have such affection for mankind of the future which is as yet non-existent; and here comes in, with all its insistence, the question of our conception of the *final* meaning or purpose of our care, and if this question in the last resort is resolved by death, if, that is to say, the final result of your progress and your culture is in any case death for each and all, then it is clear that every progressive activity of civilisation is in vain—it is aimless and senseless.

(*Here the speaker suddenly stopped, and the others turned their heads at the sound of the bell ringing at the door, and for several moments remained in astonishment. There entered into the garden, approaching the speakers with unsteady gait—the Prince.*)

LADY.—Oh! But we have not yet even begun about Antichrist.

PRINCE.—That does not matter. I have changed my mind, and I am convinced that I ought not to have expressed disapprobation of the errors of my friends without having listened to their justification.

LADY (*in a triumphant tone to the General*).—Well, you see. What now?

GENERAL (*dryly*).—Humph.

MR. Z. (*to the Prince*).—You have come very opportunely. The conversation now turns on this: is it worth while to care about progress if we know that its end is always death for every man, whether he be a savage or the furthest advanced European of the future? What would you say to that according to your theory?

PRINCE.—True Christian teaching does not even allow such a stating of the question. The Gospel solution of it is expressed with particular clearness and force in the parable of the husbandmen. The husbandmen imagined that the garden into which they were sent to work for the proprietor was their own property, that everything in the garden was made for them and that their business was only to enjoy themselves in that garden for life, forgetting about the owner and slaying those who reminded them of him and of their obligations to him. Now, nearly all people are like those husbandmen, and live in the foolish assurance that they themselves are masters of their life and that it is given to them for their enjoyment. But this is obviously foolish. Of course if we are sent here, it is at the will of someone and to some end. Now we people, we have decided that we are like mushrooms; we were born and we live only for our own pleasure; it is evident, however, that we are wrong, just as the workman would be wrong who did not carry out his master's will. Now the will of the master is expressed in the teaching of Christ. Only let people carry out this teaching, and the Kingdom of God will be established on earth and people will receive the greatest good accessible to them. Everything lies in this. *Seek ye the Kingdom of God and His Righteousness, and the rest of things will be added unto you.* We seek *the rest of things* and do not find them, and so far from establishing the Kingdom of God, we destroy it—with our various governments, armies, law courts, universities, manufactories . . .

GENERAL (*aside*).—Well, you have set up a machine!

POLITICIAN (*to the Prince*).—Have you finished?

PRINCE.—Yes.

POLITICIAN.—I must say that your solution of the question seems to me simply incomprehensible. You speak as though you were demonstrating and explaining something that you wished to press home, but meanwhile all that you say is a series of arbitrary assertions which have no connection with each other. For instance, you say: "If we are sent here it is at the will of someone and for some end." This, apparently, is your main idea, but what is there in it? Whence did you get the idea that we are sent here by someone for something? Who told you this? It is true that we exist here on the earth, but to say that our existence here is the result of being sent is simply an unproved assertion. When, for example, I was in my youth sent as an envoy, I knew it for certain, and I also knew by whom and for what I was sent. I knew, in the first place, because I had incontestable documents about it; in the second place, because I had both a personal audience with the late Emperor Alexander Nicholaevich, and personally received his Imperial instructions; and in the third place, because I received three times a year ten thousand roubles in gold. Now, if instead of all this, a strange man had come up to me in the street and announced to me that I was an envoy and was sent somewhere for some thing, I should have only begun to look round me to see whether there was not a policeman in the vicinity, to defend me from this maniac, who might —if you please—make an attempt on my life. But with regard to the case in question, when you hold no incontestable documents from your supposed master, when you have had no personal audience with him, and are receiving no salary from him, in what sense are you an envoy? Now, besides, you set down not only yourself, but all the rest as well, not only as envoys, but also as working men. By what right? I don't understand your grounds. It seems to me that this is a rhetorical improvisation *très mal inspirée d'ailleurs.*

LADY.—Now you are pretending again. You understand quite well that the Prince was not trying at all to refute your unbelief, but was stating the general Christian view that we are all dependent upon God and are bound to serve Him.

POLITICIAN.—Well, I don't understand service without salary, and if it is proved that the salary alike in all cases is death, *je présente mes compliments.*

LADY.—But, of course, you will die anyhow, no one will question that.

POLITICIAN.—Anyhow! Yes, and that proves that life is not service, and if my assent is not required for my death any more than for my birth, then I prefer to look upon death, as also life, as being merely a necessity of Nature and not to bring in the idea of some sort of service to some kind of master. But my conclusion is this: Live while you can, and strive to live as wisely and well as possible, but the condition of a wise and good life is peaceful culture. As for the rest, I assert that the so-called solution of the question which the Prince propounded on the ground of Christian teaching will not stand criticism ; but as to that let others speak who are more competent than I.

GENERAL.—What sort of a decision, indeed, have we here ? Neither solution nor statement, but only a verbal evasion of the question. It is just as though I were to invest a hostile fortress shown on a map with certain shown battalions of mine, and were then to imagine that I had captured it. This is just what happened, you know, in the famous soldiers' song :

> "The Devil carried off a quarter of us
> As we were taking the heights.
> . . . . . .
> The princes and the counts came,
> The surveyors made their maps
> On great sheets of foolscap.
> It all looked smooth on paper,
> But they forgot the precipices,
> And how to get across them."

The result of which is well known.

> "At the heights of Thediuchin
> But two companies of us arrived,
> The regiments disappeared."

PRINCE.—This is all beyond me! Is this all that you can reply to what I said ?

GENERAL.—But the point which seemed to me particularly unintelligible in what you said, was the matter of the mushrooms, as though they live for their own pleasure. I have always supposed that they live for the pleasure of those who like mushrooms in sour cream, or a mushroom pie. Now, if your Kingdom of God on earth leaves death untouched, then it follows that people will have no choice about living, and in your Kingdom of God they will live precisely as mushrooms—not the joyful mushrooms that you suppose, but real mushrooms which are fried in a frying pan. Similarly for people in your earthly Kingdom of God, everything will end one way, namely, death will devour them.

LADY.—The Prince did not say that.

GENERAL.—Not that nor anything else. What reason is there for this silence about the most important point?

MR. Z.—Before taking up this question, I should like to know what was the source of the parable in which you, Prince, expressed your view? Or is it your own composition?

PRINCE.—Composition, indeed! You know it comes from the Gospel.

MR. Z.—No, not so! There is no such parable found in any of the Gospels.

LADY.—Heaven help you! Why do you distort the Prince's meaning? You know it is the parable of the husbandmen in the Gospel.

MR. Z.—Superficially it is somewhat like it, but altogether different both in tenor and meaning.

LADY.—What do you mean? Hold hard. It seems to me to be entirely the same parable. As you reason so subtly, I don't trust a word of what you say.

Mr. Z.—You needn't; I have the book in my pocket. (*Here he took out a small copy of the New Testament and began to turn over the leaves.*) The parable of the husbandmen is found in three Gospels: Matthew, Mark, and Luke; there is no material difference between the three texts. So it will do to read it over in one Gospel—the most detailed—Luke. It is in the twentieth chapter, which contains the last and final discourse of Christ to the people. Things were drawing to a close, and here it is related (end of the nineteenth and beginning of the twentieth chapter) how the adversaries of Christ—the parties of the High Priests and the Scribes—made decided attacks on Him, publicly requesting that He should show the full extent of His activity, and say by what right and by what authority He was acting. But, excuse me, I had better read it (*reading*): " And He taught daily in the temple. But the chief priests and the scribes and the chief of the people sought to destroy Him, and could not find what they might do: for all the people were very attentive to hear Him. And it came to pass that on one of those days, as He taught the people in the temple, and preached the Gospel, the chief priests and the scribes came upon Him, with the elders, and spake unto Him, saying, Tell us by what authority doest Thou these things? or who is He that gave Thee this authority? And He answered and said unto them, I will also ask you one thing; and answer Me: The baptism of John, was it from heaven, or of men? And they reasoned with themselves, saying, if we shall say, From Heaven; He will say, Why then believed you him not? But and if we say, Of men; all the people will stone us: for they be persuaded that John was a prophet. And they answered, that they could not tell whence it was. And Jesus said unto them, Neither tell I you by what authority I do these things."

LADY.—Why do you read this? It is good that Christ did not answer when they questioned Him; but what has this to do with the husbandmen?

MR. Z.—Wait; it is all one thing. You were wrong in saying that Christ did not answer. He answered quite definitely and twice over; He pointed to His activities as a witness which His questioners could not reject, and besides, He proved that they themselves had no power or right over Him, since they acted only from dread of the people and conformed to the opinions of the crowd only from fear of their lives. But, of course, a real power is one which does not follow after others, but leads others after itself. In fearing and listening to the people, these men showed that the real power had left them and become the property of the people. Christ now turns to them in order to accuse them before the people of opposition to Himself. The whole purport of the Gospel parable of the husbandmen, as you yourselves will see directly, is to show up the national leaders of the Jews as unfit because of their resistance to the Messiah. (*He reads:*) "Then began He to speak to the people this parable: A certain man planted a vineyard, and let it forth to husbandmen, and went into a far country for a long time. And at the season, he sent a servant to the husbandmen, that they should give him of the fruit of the vineyard ; but the husbandmen beat him, and sent him away empty. And again he sent another servant : and they beat him also, and entreated him shamefully, and sent him away empty. And again he sent a third : and they wounded him also, and cast him out. Then said the lord of the vineyard, What shall I do ? I will send my beloved son : it may be they will reverence him, when they see him. But when the husbandmen saw him, they reasoned among themselves, saying, ' This is the heir ; come, let us kill him, that the inheritance may be ours.' So they cast him out of the vineyard, and killed him. What therefore shall the lord of the vineyard do unto them ? He shall come and destroy these husbandmen, and shall give the vineyard to others. And when they heard it, they said, God forbid. And He beheld them, and said, What is this then that is written, The stone which the builders rejected, the same is become the head of the corner ? Whosoever shall fall upon that stone shall be broken ; but on whomsoever it shall fall, it will grind him to powder. And the chief priests and the scribes the same hour sought to lay hands on Him ; and they feared the people ; for they perceived that He had spoken this parable against them." Now, I ask, about whom and what was the parable of the husbandmen spoken ?

PRINCE.—I do not understand what is your objection here ? The Jewish Chief Priests and Scribes were offended because they were and acknowledged themselves to be, counterparts of those bad worldly people mentioned in the parable.

Mr. Z.—But of what, in particular, were they convicted here?

Prince.—Of not fulfilling the true teaching.

Politician.—It is clear the scoundrels lived like mushrooms for their own pleasure, they smoked tobacco, drank vodka, ate carrion and also offered of it to their God, they married, presided in law courts and took part in wars.

Lady.—Do you think that it is worthy of your age and position to mock in this way? Do not listen to him, Prince. We want to speak seriously with you. Tell me this; in the Gospel parable, you know, the husbandmen perish because they murdered the owner's son and heir — and this is the main thing according to the Gospel—why do you pass over it?

Prince.—I let it pass because it refers to the personal fate of Christ, which no doubt has its own importance and interest, but all the same is not essential for the one thing necessary.

Lady.—That is?

Prince.—That is, for the fulfilment of the Gospel teaching, by which the Kingdom of God and His Righteousness are attained.

Lady.—Wait a moment; I have something all confused in my head—what exactly is it?—Yes (*to Mr. Z.*), you have the Gospel in your hands, so tell us, please, what comes in this chapter after the parable?

Mr. Z. (*turning over the leaves of the little book*).— There comes the bit about rendering to Cæsar what is due to him, next about the resurrection of the dead, that the dead will rise because God is not the God of the dead but of the living, and after that, it is proved that Christ is not the son of David but the Son of God—well, and the two last verses are against the hypocrisy and boasting of the Scribes.

LADY.—There, you see, Prince! And this also is Gospel teaching; that we must acknowledge the state in worldly matters, we must believe in the resurrection of the dead, and also that Christ is not a mere man but the Son of God.

PRINCE.—But how can it be possible to conclude this from one chapter of uncertain authorship and date?

LADY.—Ah, no! I know at once, and without looking, that it is not only one chapter, but in all four Gospels there is a great deal both about the resurrection and about the Divinity of Christ—especially in St. John, and they read it at funerals.

MR. Z.—But about that, though it is of uncertain authorship and date, still free German criticism has now acknowledged that all four Gospels are of apostolic origin, of the first century.

POLITICIAN.—Yes, and in the thirteenth edition of " Vie de Jésus " I noticed a recantation with regard to the fourth Gospel.

MR. Z.—It is impossible to go back upon our teachers. But the great misfortune, Prince, is that, whatever our four Gospels may be, when and by whom they may have been put together, there does not exist another gospel which you would find more worthy of credit and more harmonious with your teaching.

GENERAL.—What! There is not another? But there is a fifth in which there is nothing about Christ and only a *teaching* with reference to slaughter and warfare.

LADY.—Are you at it too? Shame on you! You know that the more you and your ally, the official, tease the Prince, the more I shall take his part. I am sure, Prince, that you wish to take Christianity on its very best side, and that your Gospel, though it is not the same as ours, aims at that also; just as in old days they wrote books called " L'Esprit de M. de Montesquieu," " L'Esprit de Fénélon," so you or your teachers have wished to write " L'Esprit de l'Évangile." The pity is that no one of your way of thinking has written any book which could be called " The Spirit of Christianity according to the teaching of So and So." It is essential for you to have something in the way of a catechism in order that we simple people may not lose the thread in all these intricacies. At one time we hear that the main point is in the Sermon on the Mount, at another time they suddenly tell us that before all things it is necessary to labour in the sweat of one's brow at agriculture—though there is nothing about that in the Gospel, but it's in Genesis, in the same place as " in sorrow thou shalt bring forth children "— but this is not a commandment, it is only an unhappy destiny; at another time they say that it is necessary to give all to the poor, and again to give nothing to anybody, because money is evil and it is not good to do evil to others, but only to one's self and one's family, and that for others it is only necessary to labour ; then again they say : do nothing but only meditate ; again they say : the vocation of woman is to bear as many healthy children as possible—but then suddenly—nothing of that is at all necessary ; next, not to eat meat is the first step, but why the first nobody knows ; next, no vodka or tobacco ; next, pancakes ; and then it is military service that is the chief evil, and the chief duty of the Christian is to refuse it, and anyone who is not carried off for a soldier is, of course, for that reason a saint. Perhaps I am talking nonsense, but it's not my fault. It is impossible to make all this out.

PRINCE.—I also think it is essential for us to have an intelligent summing up of the true teaching. I fancy it is being actually prepared.

LADY.—Well, and while it is being prepared, tell us now in two words what is the essential point of the Gospel in your opinion.

PRINCE.—It seems clearly, that it is the great principle of not opposing evil by force.

POLITICIAN.—And how then will you get rid of tobacco ?

PRINCE.—Get rid of tobacco ?

POLITICIAN.—Oh ! Good heavens ! What connection is there, I ask, between the principle of non-resistance to evil and the demand of abstinence from tobacco, wine, meat, and sexual intercourse ?

PRINCE.—The connection, I think, is clear : all these vicious habits stupefy a man—they overpower in him the demands of his reason or conscience. This is why soldiers generally go off drunk to war.

Mr. Z.—Particularly to an unsuccessful war. But we can leave that. The principle of non-resistance to evil is important in itself; does it justify or not ascetic demands? According to you, if we cease to resist evil by force, then evil will at once disappear. That means, it subsists only through our resistance, or in consequence of the means we take against it, but it has no real strength of its own. In reality there is no evil, it appears only in consequence of our false theory in supposing that evil exists and in acting on that supposition. Is it not so?

Prince.—Of course it is.

Mr. Z.—But if in reality there is no evil how do you explain the surprising failure of the work of Christ in history? From your point of view, it has not altogether succeeded, as after all nothing came of it, or rather there came of it in every case much more harm than good.

Prince.—How so?

Mr. Z.—What a strange question! Well, if this is unintelligible to you, we will go into it in detail. Christ, even according to you, preached true good more clearly, forcibly and consistently than anyone. Is it so?

Prince.—Yes.

Mr. Z.—And true good consists in not opposing evil with force, that is, so-called evil, since there is no actual evil.

Prince.—Yes.

Mr. Z.—Christ not only preached, but Himself fulfilled to the end the demands of this good, undergoing without resistance a death of torment.

Christ, according to you, died and did not rise again. Very well. After His example many thousands of His followers endured the same. Very well. And what, in your opinion, was the result of all this?

PRINCE.—Would you wish that some shining angels should set garlands on these martyrs and place them somewhere in tents in the gardens of Paradise as a reward for their heroism?

MR. Z.—No, why do you ask that? Of course, both you and I, I dare say, would wish for all our dear ones, both living and dead, the very best and most pleasant thing possible. But we are not concerned with our own desires, but with what you think actually resulted from the preaching and heroic acts of Christ and His followers.

PRINCE.—Resulted for whom? For them?

MR. Z.—Well, for them doubtless the result was a death of torment; but they, of course, in their moral heroism, submitted to it willingly and not in order to receive shining crowns for themselves, but in order to remit real good to others, to all mankind. So this is what I ask you, what good did the heroic martyrdom of these people do to others, to all mankind? According to an old saying, the blood of the martyrs is the seed of the Church. This is true to fact, but in your opinion the Church brought about such a distortion of true Christianity that it was forthwith quite forgotten among men, and after eighteen centuries it all had to be recovered from the beginning without any guarantee of better success, that is, in an altogether hopeless way.

PRINCE.—Why hopeless?

Mr. Z.—Well, I suppose you do not deny that Christ and the first generations of Christians put all their whole soul into the thing and gave up their lives for it, and if, nevertheless, there was no result, as you suppose, then on what can you base any hopes of a different outcome? There is only one undoubted and permanent end of all this matter, which is absolutely the same whether for those who originate it, or for those who distort and ruin it, or for those who recover it; they all, according to you, died in the past, they die in the present, they will die in the future, and out of good actions, out of true preaching, nothing except death ever did happen, does happen, or promises to happen. What then does it all come to? What an eccentricity; evil which is non-existent always triumphs, and good always relapses into nothingness.

Lady.—Do the bad people then not die?

Mr. Z.—Very much so, but the point is, that by the kingdom of death the strength of evil only is confirmed, while the strength of good, on the contrary, is disproved. And, indeed, evil is obviously stronger than good, and if the obvious counts as the only real thing, then one must reckon the world as a fundamentally evil affair. But how people can grow wise while standing exclusively on the ground of obvious and current reality, and consequently acknowledging the obvious preponderance of evil over good, and at the same time assert that there is no evil, and that consequently there is no need to struggle with it—that is a thing that I with my intellect do not understand, and I am looking for help from the side of the Prince.

Politician.—Well, to begin with, tell us your way out of the difficulty.

Mr. Z.—It seems to me simple. Evil in fact exists, and it is expressed not in a mere absence of good, but in a positive opposition and preponderance of lower qualities over high in all the provinces of existence. There is individual evil—it expresses itself in the fact that the lower side of man, the bestial and brutal passions, resist the better tendencies of the soul, and *overcome them* in an enormous majority of people. There is general evil—consisting in the fact that the popular crowd, being as individuals enslaved by evil, opposes the salutary efforts of the few better people and overcomes them. There is, lastly, physical evil in man—in that the lower material elements of his body oppose the vital and living force that joins them together in the beautiful form of the organism, and break up this form by destroying the effective foundation of everything higher. This is the extreme evil called death; and if it were necessary to acknowledge the victory of this extreme physical evil as final and absolute, then it would be impossible to count as serious progress any so-called victories of good in the province of personal or general morality. Even if we suppose that a man of good, Socrates, let us say, triumphed not only over his inward enemies—the bad passions—but that he also succeeded in convincing and reforming his public enemies, and in transforming Greek politics—what advantage is this ephemeral and superficial victory over evil, if evil triumphs finally in the deepest stratum of existence over the very foundations of life? Both to the reformer and to the reformed there is one and the same end—death. How could one logically put a high value on the moral victories of the Socratic good over the moral microbes of bad passions in his own breast, and over the public microbes of the market place of Athens, if the real victory was found to lie with the far worse, lower, coarser microbes of physical decomposition? Then no moral formula could protect us against extreme pessimism and despair.

POLITICIAN.—We have already heard that. But, for you, what is there to rely on against despair?

MR. Z.—We have one thing to rely on—an actual resurrection. We know that the struggle of good with evil takes place not only in the soul and in society, but lower down in the physical world. As to that we already know up to now of one victory gained by the good element in life—in the personal resurrection of One, and we look for future victories in the collective resurrection of all. So even evil finds its explanation, or the final exposition of its existence in the fact that it wholly conduces to greater and greater triumph, realisation, and reinforcement of good; if death is stronger than mortal life, then the resurrection to eternal life is stronger than the one or the other. The Kingdom of God is the kingdom of life, triumphing through resurrection over life, wherein is actual, realised and final good. In that Kingdom is all the power and all the work of

Christ, in it is His effective love to us and ours to Him. Everything else is merely—conditions, ways, methods. If there is no belief in the accomplished resurrection of One, and no hope of a future resurrection of all, you can only talk in word about any sort of Kingdom of God, but in fact there stands out only a kingdom of death.

PRINCE.—How is that?

MR. Z.—Well, you not only admit (as everyone does), *the fact* of death, *i.e.*, the fact that people in general have died, do die, and still will die—but you further exalt this into an absolute law, to which there is no single exception, and you hold that this is the world in which death is for ever an absolute law. Then how can you call this world anything except a kingdom of death? And what is your Kingdom of God on earth except an arbitrary and vain euphemism for the kingdom of death?

POLITICIAN.—I also think it is vain, because you must not change a known magnitude into an unknown. No one has ever seen God, and what kind of a Kingdom His may be—is unknown to anyone; but the death of people and animals we have all seen and we know it as the supreme power in the world from which no one can escape. So what is the good of putting instead of this a, some sort of an x? You will accomplish nothing by this, except it be the confusing and deluding of your " small people."

PRINCE.—I do not understand what we are now discussing. Death is a phenomenon, certainly very interesting, you can if you like call it a law, as being a phenomenon constant amongst earthly creatures and unavoidable by any of them; you can also speak of the absoluteness of that law, since, hitherto, there has been no clearly established exception; but what real or vital importance can all that have for the true Christian teaching, which speaks to us through our conscience only about one thing: namely, what we ought and what we ought not to do *here* and *now*? It is clear that the voice of conscience can refer only to that which it is in our power to do or not to do. Therefore, conscience not only says nothing to us about death, but cannot say anything. With all its immense importance for our human earthly feelings and desires, death is not subject to our will and therefore it cannot have any moral importance for us. In that respect—and that is the only thing of importance at the moment—death is a purely indifferent fact, just as much as bad weather, for example. Because I acknowledge the inevitable periodical occurrence of bad weather and more or less suffer from it, am I therefore bound to say, instead of the Kingdom of God, the kingdom of bad weather?

MR. Z.—No, you are not; in the first place, because bad weather has its kingdom only in Petersburg and we have come here with you to the Mediterranean and laugh at its kingdom; and secondly, your simile does not fit because one can praise God even in bad weather and feel one's self in His Kingdom, while the dead, as is said in the Scriptures, praise not God; also because, as his Excellency remarked, it is more suitable to call this sorrowful world the kingdom of death than the Kingdom of God.

Lady.—Well, now you are all on names—this is tedious. Is it then a matter of names? Tell us instead, please, what you really understand by the Kingdom of God and His Righteousness?

Prince.—I understand a condition of people in which they act only with a clear conscience and so fulfil the will of God, which enjoins on them only one clear good.

Mr. Z.—But further, the voice of conscience, according to you, speaks only about the fulfilment of duty *now* and *here*.

Prince.—Of course.

Mr. Z.—Well, but is it the case that your conscience is entirely silent about a breach of duty that you were guilty of, let us say in your youth, with regard to people now long dead?

Prince.—In that case, the point of these reminders is in this: that I should not do anything of that sort *now*.

Mr. Z.—Well, that's not quite so, but it's not worth while quarrelling about. I only want to remind you of another and more incontestable sphere of conscience. Long ago the moralists compared the voice of conscience to that genius or demon which accompanied Socrates, warning him against undutiful conduct, but never pointing out positively what he ought to do. Exactly the same thing may be said of conscience.

Prince.—How is that so? Does not conscience then suggest to me, for example, that I should help my neighbour when I know he is in a position of want or danger?

WAR AND CHRISTIANITY

MR. Z.—It is very pleasant to hear this from you. But, if you analyse carefully such a position you will see that the *rôle* of conscience, even here, proves to be entirely negative ; it demands of you merely that you should not remain inactive or indifferent in face of someone else's need, but how precisely you ought to act on his behalf, conscience itself does not tell you.

PRINCE.—Just so, because this depends on the circumstances of the case, on my position and on that of the man I ought to help.

MR. Z.—Of course, but the estimate and consideration of these circumstances and conditions is not the business of the conscience but of the mind.

PRINCE.—But how is it possible to separate reason from conscience ?

MR. Z.—To separate them is not necessary ; but you must distinguish, and for this reason, because in reality there sometimes arises not only separation, but opposition between the mind and the conscience. If they were one and the same, then in what way would the intellect be able to be of service in matters not only foreign to morality, but directly immoral ? But you know this happens. Of course, it is possible to give help, acting from the mind and not from the conscience ; for example, supposing I give food and drink and show every kindness to a necessitous man in order to make him an accomplice such as I require for the successful execution of some sort of swindle or other bad deed.

PRINCE.—Well, yes, this is elementary. But what do you deduce therefrom ?

Mr. Z.—Why this. If the voice of conscience, with all its proper significance as a warner and reproacher, does not give positive practical and definite directions for our action, and our free will stands in need of the mind as an assisting instrument, and if meanwhile the mind shows itself to be a doubtful servant for it, since it is capable and ready to serve two masters—good and evil—then for the fulfilment of the will of God and the attaining of the Kingdom of God, besides the conscience and the mind, yet a certain third thing is necessary.

Prince.—What is that in your opinion?

Mr. Z.—To put it shortly, it is the *inspiration of good*, or a direct and positive action of the best principle upon us and in us. In such a joint action, both mind and conscience become trusty helpers of the good itself, and morality, instead of being a good behaviour, which is always questionable, becomes an unquestionable life lived in the good itself—becomes the organic development and completion of the whole of man—within and without, individual and society, people and mankind, so as to come to its climax in a living unity formed of the revived past together with the evolving future in the eternal present of the Kingdom of God, which will indeed be on earth, but only on a new earth which is lovingly united to a new heaven.

Prince.—I have nothing against such poetical metaphors, but why do you suppose that people who are fulfilling the will of God according to the Gospel commandments lack what you call the inspiration of good?

Mr. Z.—Partly because I do not see in them any active signs of that inspiration, any free, excessive transports of love—because, you know, God giveth not the spirit by measure—also, I do not see a joyful and contented repose arising from a sense of possessing these gifts, though only in an elementary form; but chiefly I presuppose in you a lack of the religious inspiration, because in your opinion it is unnecessary. If the good consists solely in the fulfilment of " a will " where is there any room left for inspiration? A rule when once for all laid down is definite and identical for all. He who gave the rule died long ago, and according to you did not rise, and for us He has no personal living existence; but an absolute primordial good presents itself to you, not as the father of lights and spirits, who can directly enlighten and inspire you, but as a calculating master who has sent you, a hireling, to work in his vineyard, while he himself lives somewhere away and sends to you from there for his fruits.

Prince.—You seem to think that we invented this figure arbitrarily.

Mr. Z.—No, but you arbitrarily see in it the highest force of the relation between man and God in arbitrarily excluding from the Gospel text the very substance of it. Which is to point to the son and heir in whom is found the true living type of the relation between God and man. It is a case of a master, obligations to a master, and the will of a master. But this is what I have to say to you in reply : As long as your master only lays obligations upon you, and claims from you the fulfilment of his will, I do not see how you can prove to me that this master is a real master and not an impostor.

PRINCE.—That's very nice, and supposing I know, both in conscience and reason, that the demands of the master are simply expressive of the purest form of good.

MR. Z.—I am sorry; I am not speaking of that. I do not dispute that the master demands good of you; but does it follow that he is himself good?

PRINCE.—Why, how's that?

MR. Z.—How strange. I always thought that the quality of goodness in anybody is not shown by what he demands of others but by what he does himself. If this is not clear to you logically, then here's an actual historical example for you. The Muscovite Tsar Ivan IV., in his well-known letter, demanded of Prince Andrew Kurbscki that he should display the greatest good and highest moral heroism by refusing resistance to evil and simply submitting himself to a martyr's death for the truth. This will of the master was good in what it demanded of another, only it did not in any way prove that the master who demanded such good was himself good. It is clear that, although martyrdom for the truth is the highest moral good, yet this does not imply anything in defence of Ivan IV., seeing that he was in this instance not the martyr but the cause of martyrdom.

PRINCE.—What do you mean by this?

MR. Z.—I mean, that so long as you do not show me the good quality of your master in his own deeds, but only in his verbal instructions to his workmen,

I remain of my opinion that this far-away master of yours, demanding good of others, but doing nothing good himself, imposing obligations, but showing no love, never appearing for you to see, but living somewhere away incognito—that he is none other than the *God of this world* . . .

GENERAL.—What an accursed incognito!

LADY.—Ah, do not say so! How terrible! The Power of the Cross defend us. (*She crosses herself.*)

PRINCE.—It was possible earlier on to foresee something of this kind.

MR. Z.—I have no doubt, Prince, that you, through an honest mistake, accept a clever impostor as the true God. The *cleverness* of the impostor is, for you, a great extenuating circumstance; I myself have not analysed how the matter stands; but at present I have no doubt whatever, and you will understand with what feelings I must regard what I consider to be a deceitful and seductive *personal* good.

LADY.—This, you know, is rather insulting.

PRINCE.—I assure you I am not in the least offended. A general and very interesting question was put, and it is strange to me that my interlocutor apparently imagines that this question has to do with me only, and not with himself as well. You demand of me that I should show you the really good deeds of my master, which are witnesses of the fact that he is the origin of good and not evil. Well, will you yourselves show me any good deed of your master which I would not be able to ascribe to mine?

GENERAL.—You know, one deed has already been shown upon which all the others rest.

PRINCE.—What exactly?

MR. Z.—The real victory over evil in a real resurrection. Only by this, I repeat, is revealed the true Kingdom of God. For without that there is only the kingdom of death and sin, and of their creator, the devil. The resurrection—only not in a figurative sense, but in a real one—that is the proof of the true God.

PRINCE.—Yes, if it pleases you to believe in such mythology. I, you know, ask you for facts which are capable of proof and not for your beliefs.

MR. Z.—Not so fast, Prince. We both start from one faith, or, if you like, one mythology—only I pursue it to the end, while you, in spite of logic, remain arbitrarily at the beginning of the way. You admit the power of good and its ultimate triumph on earth, don't you?

PRINCE.—I admit it.

MR. Z.—What is it; fact or belief?

PRINCE.—Reasonable belief.

MR. Z.—Let us see. Reason, as we were taught in the Seminary, demands, among other things, that nothing is to be admitted without adequate foundation. Tell me, then, please, upon what adequate foundation, having admitted the power of good in moral improvement and in the perfecting of man and humanity, you admit that good is powerless against death?

PRINCE.—I think it is necessary for you to say why you ascribe to good some sort of power beyond the confines of the moral sphere.

Mr. Z.—I will tell you. When once I believe in good, and in its peculiar power, and that the very conception of this good power implies its actual and *absolute* superiority, then I logically admit such a power as boundless, and nothing will prevent me from believing in the truth of the resurrection which has been attested *historically*. Besides, if you had said frankly from the very beginning that the Christian *faith* was nothing to you, that its matter was mythological to you, then I, of course, should have restrained myself from expressing that animosity to your manner of thought, which I was not able to hide from you; for bearing animosity towards people for their theoretical errors means acknowledging oneself to be small in mind, weak in faith and bad at heart. Every one who really believes and at the same time is free from an excess of stupidity, faint-heartedness and heartlessness must look with sincere goodwill on any adversary and denier of religious truth who is frank, open and, in short, honest. At the present time this is such a rarity that it is difficult for me to tell you with what special pleasure I look upon a declared enemy of Christianity. I am almost prepared to see in every one of them a future Apostle Paul, while in some zealots for Christianity I involuntarily seem to see Judas the traitor. But you, Prince, have so openly declared yourself that I absolutely refuse to number you amongst the present countless male and female Judases, and already I foresee the moment in which I shall feel towards you the same good disposition which many declared atheists and non-Christians have aroused in me.

Politician.—Well, since now it is so happily explained that neither these atheists and non-Christians nor such " true Christians " as the Prince here represent Antichrist, the time has come at last for you to show us his real portrait.

Mr. Z.—That's what you are after! But are you satisfied with even one of the many representations of Christ which have been made at any time by talented artists? I do not know one representation that is satisfactory. I suppose there cannot be one, for the reason that Christ is individual and unique in His way, and consequently an incarnation unlike any other of His essential nature—namely, good. To represent this is unattainable by any artistic genius. But the same thing must be said about Antichrist. He is likewise individual and unique, a full and complete embodiment of evil. It is impossible to show his portrait. In Church literature we find only his passport, with general and particular remarks.

Lady.—His portrait isn't necessary. God forbid! You had better explain why he himself is necessary in your opinion, what his work really is, and if he will come soon.

Mr. Z.—Well, I am able to satisfy you better than you think. Some years ago one of my fellow-students in the Academy, who afterwards became a monk, when he was dying, bequeathed to me a manuscript of his which he valued highly, but was unwilling and unable to print. He calls it, " A Short Narrative about Antichrist." Although it takes the form of fiction, or the appearance of an historical picture, imagined in advance, this work, in my opinion, gives all that in the highest probability can be said about this subject in accordance with the Holy Scriptures, ecclesiastical tradition, and sound reason.

POLITICIAN.—I suppose it is not the production of our acquaintance, Varsonophia?

MR. Z.—No, his name was one of far more refinement, Pansophia.

POLITICIAN.—Pan Sophia. A Pole?

MR. Z.—Not at all; one of the Russian clericals. If you will permit me to go up to my room for a moment I will bring this manuscript and read it through. It isn't long.

LADY.—Go by all means, only do not get lost. (*While Mr. Z. goes to his room for the manuscript all get up and walk about the garden.*)

POLITICIAN.—I do not know what it is; either my eyesight is dimmed by old age, or something has happened in nature. Only, I notice that there are now no longer in any season, or in any place, any more of those bright and quite clear days, which formerly there were in all climates. Take to-day; not a cloud; we are far enough from the sea, and yet everything, as it were, is covered with something—something fine and intangible, and there is no absolute clearness. Have you noticed it, General?

GENERAL.—I have noticed it for many years.

LADY.—And I, for this past year, have begun to

notice it also. Not only in the air but in the soul: for here there is no " absolute clearness," as you say. Everywhere there is some sort of alarm, as if it were a foreboding of some evil. I am sure that you, Prince, feel the same thing.

PRINCE.—No, I have noticed nothing special. The air seems as usual.

GENERAL.—But you are too young to notice any difference. You have no means of comparison. How can you remember? But when you look back over fifty years you feel something.

PRINCE.—I think the first supposition is correct. It is a phenomenon of weak eyesight.

POLITICIAN.—We are growing old undoubtedly; but neither is the earth growing younger; a double weariness is felt.

GENERAL.—More probably it is the devil driving a mist with his tail across God's light. Also a sign of Antichrist.

LADY (*pointing out Mr. Z., who was descending the terrace*).—We shall soon know all about it.

(*They all sit down in their former places and Mr. Z. begins to read the manuscript he has brought with him.*)

SHORT NARRATIVE ABOUT ANTICHRIST.

Pan-mongolism! Although the name is wild,
I find some consolation in the sound,
A mystical premonition, as it were,
Of the glorious providence of God.

LADY.—Where does this heading come from? Whence this epigraph?

Mr. Z.—I think, the author wrote it himself.

Lady.—Well, read on.

Mr. Z. (*reads*).—The twentieth century after the birth of Christ was the period of the last great wars, civil dissension and revolutions. The very greatest of foreign wars had as its remote cause, the intellectual movement of Pan-mongolism which arose in Japan towards the end of the nineteenth century. The imitative Japanese, with astonishing rapidity and success, copied the material forms of European culture and adopted certain European ideas of a lower order. Having learned from newspapers and historical text-books about the existence in the West of Pan-hellenism, Pan-germanism, Pan-slavism, Pan-islamism, they proclaimed the great idea of Pan-mongolism, which was the gathering into one, under their leadership, of all the peoples of Eastern Asia with the object of making a resolute struggle against foreigners, that is to say, Europeans. Taking advantage of the fact that Europe was engaged in a final and decisive struggle with the Moslem world in the beginning of the twentieth century, they began the realisation of a great plan—first, the occupation of Korea, then that of Peking, where, with the help of the progressive party in China, they would depose the ancient Manchurian dynasty and put the Japanese in its place. The Chinese Conservatives soon came to an agreement with them. They saw that of two evils it was better to choose the lesser and therefore, blood being thicker than water, they necessarily chose their brothers the Japanese.

The government of China had not the power to hold its ground and would have unavoidably become subject either to the Europeans or to the Japanese. But it was clear that the Japanese sovereignty, abolishing the external forms of Chinese dominion which seemed eminently trivial, would not affect the intimate foundations of national life, whilst on the other hand the predominance of the European powers, who supported, for political reasons, the Christian missionaries, would threaten the deepest spiritual foundations of China. The former national hatred of the Chinese for the Japanese had arisen at a time when neither the one nor the other had known Europeans, in the presence of whom this enmity of two related peoples became mere civil dissension, and lost any significance. Europeans were entirely foreigners, merely enemies, and their domination could in no way be flattering to race pride, whilst in the hands of Japan, the Chinese saw the delightful lure of Pan-mongolism, which, moreover, in their eyes did away with the sad inevitability of European influence. "You see, O obstinate brothers," said the Japanese, "that we take the arms of the Western dogs, not from any infatuation for them, but simply to beat them with their own weapons. If you join us and accept our practical guidance we shall not only quickly drive the white devils out of our Asia, but we shall fight them in their own countries and found a real middle kingdom over the whole world. You are right in your national pride and contempt of Europeans, but it is vain to nourish these feelings on dreams alone without intelligent activity. In this we have surpassed you and we must show you the way of our common welfare. Otherwise, see for yourselves what your policy of self-assurance and distrust of us, your natural friends and defenders, has given you: Russia and England, Germany and France have almost shared you between them, leaving you nothing, and all your tigerish plots show only the weak end of a serpent's tail." Reasonable Chinamen found this sound, and the Japanese dynasty pronounced it well founded. Its first care, of course, was the creation of a powerful army and navy. A great part of the fighting forces of Japan was brought to China, where it composed the staff of an enormous new army. Japanese officers speaking Chinese acted as instructors far more successfully than the Europeans who had been dismissed, and in the countless populations of China, Manchuria, Mongolia and Tibet was found a sufficiency of excellent military material. Already the first Chinese Emperor of the Japanese dynasty was able to make a successful trial of the arms of the revived empire, driving out the French from Tonkin and Siam, the English from Burma, and including in the Middle Empire all of Indo-China. His heir, Chinese on his mother's side, thus uniting in himself both the cunning and elasticity of the Chinese with the energy, mobility and enterprise of the Japanese, mobilised in Chinese Turkestan an army of four millions, and at the time that the Tsun-li-Yamin confidently informed the Russian Ambassador that this force was intended for the conquest of India, the Emperor appears in our Central Asia, and having collected there all the inhabitants, moves swiftly across the Urals and swamps with his armies all Eastern and Central Russia, whilst the Russian forces, hastily mobilised in various parts, hurry from Poland, from Lithuania, from Kiev, Volhynia, Petersburg and Finland. Owing to the absence of a prearranged plan of campaign and the enormous numerical superiority of the enemy, the fighting qualities of the Russian forces allow them only to perish with honour. The swiftness of the invasion left no time for the necessary concentration, and army corps after army corps was exterminated in hard and hopeless conflicts. The Mongols did not come off cheaply, but they easily replaced their losses, having control of all the Asiatic railways, while a Russian army of two hundred thousand, for a long time concentrated on the Manchurian frontier, made an unsuccessful attempt to invade a well-defended China. Having left a part of his forces in Russia to prevent the forming of new armies, and also for the pursuit of guerilla bands which had increased in number, the Emperor with three armies crossed the German frontier. Here they had succeeded in making preparations, and one of the Mongol armies was annihilated. At this time the party of a belated *revanche* was in power in France and a million hostile bayonets quickly appeared at the Germans' back. Having fallen between the anvil and the hammer, the German army was forced to accept honourable conditions of surrender proposed by the Emperor. The jubilant French fraternising with the yellow faces were scattered throughout Germany, and soon lost every appearance of military discipline. The Emperor commanded his soldiers to kill the more unnecessary of his allies, which was accomplished with Chinese accuracy. In Paris an uprising of working men *sans patrie* took place, and the capital of western culture opened its gates to the Conqueror of the East. Having satisfied his curiosity, the Emperor set out for Boulogne, where, under cover of the fleet which had come from the Pacific, he got ready transports to convey his army to Great Britain. But he was in need of money, and the English bought their freedom for a milliard pounds. For a year all the European Powers acknowledged themselves vassals of the Emperor, who, having left a sufficient army of occupation in Europe, returned to the East, where he began preparations for a naval expedition against America and Australia. For half a century Europe lay under the Mongol yoke. In the domain of thought this epoch was remarkable for a general blending and mutual interchange of European and Eastern ideas, a repetition *en grand* of the ancient Alexandrian syncritism. In the practical domain of life, three phenomena became in the highest degree characteristic: the large influx into Europe of Chinese and Japanese labour, and in consequence of this the violent embitterment of the social-economic question; the series of palliative attempts to solve this question, which were prolonged on the part of the governing classes; and the increasing international activity of secret social organisations which resulted in a widespread European plot to drive out the Mongols and to re-establish the independence of Europe. This colossal plot, into which the local national governments entered so far as they were able, being under the control of the Imperial viceroys, was prepared in a masterly and succeeded in a brilliant manner. At an appointed time began the slaughter of the Mongol soldiers and the murder and expulsion of the workmen. In all places secret staffs of the European army appeared, and a general mobilisation took place according to a long-prepared and circumstantial plan. The new Emperor, the grandson of the great Conqueror, hastened from China to Russia, but here his numberless hordes were annihilated by the all-European army. Their scattered remnants returned to the depths of Asia, and Europe became free. If the half century of subjugation to the Asiatic barbarians was the result of the disunion of the Powers, who thought only of their separate national interests, a great and glorious liberation was attained by the international organisation of the united forces of all the peoples of Europe.

As a natural consequence of this obvious fact it followed that the old traditional order of divided nations everywhere lost its significance, and almost everywhere the last traces of monarchical institutions disappeared. Europe in the twenty-first century presented a union of more or less democratic States—the United States of Europe. The progress of external culture, somewhat retarded by the Mongol invasion and war of liberation, again went forward. Matters of internal consciousness—questions of life and death, of the last judgment, of the world and of mankind, complicated and confused by a multitude of new physiological and psychological investigations and discoveries remained as formerly, insoluble. Only one important negative result was made clear—the absolute fall of theoretical materialism. The representation of the universe as a system of floating atoms, and of life as the result of a mechanical agglomeration of minute alterations of matter—such a statement no longer satisfied even one thinking being. Mankind had for ever outgrown this stage of philosophical youthfulness. But it was clear on the other hand that it had also outgrown the youthful capacity of a simple and unconscious belief. The idea that God created the universe out of nothing, etc., ceased to be taught even in the primary schools. A certain general and higher level of representing such matters had been worked out, below which no dogmatism could fall. And if the vast majority of thinking people remained entirely unbelievers, the few who believed became of necessity " thinkers," fulfilling the instructions of the apostle : be children at heart but not in mind.

There was at this time among the few people believing in spiritual things a remarkable man—called by many a superman—who was, however, as far from being intellectual as from being a child at heart. He was still young, but, thanks to his great talent, at thirty-three years of age was widely proclaimed as a great thinker, writer, and social worker. Being conscious within himself of great spiritual power he had been always a convinced spiritualist, and his clear understanding always showed him the truth of that in which one must believe—Good, God, the Messiah. In these he *believed*, but he *loved only himself.* He believed in God, but, in the depths of his soul, he involuntarily and unconsciously preferred himself to Him. He believed in Good, but the All Seeing Eye of the Eternal knew that this man bowed before the power of evil when it offered him a bribe—not by the snare of the senses and lower passions, nor even by the superior attraction of power, but through his immeasurable self-love alone. Besides, this self-love was neither an unconscious instinct nor a foolish pretence. In view of his exceptional talent, his beauty, nobility of character, his supreme display of continence, his disinterestedness, and his active beneficence, it seemed that his enormous self-love was justifiable, and worthy of a great spiritualist, ascetic, and philanthropist. Was he to blame?—a man so plenteously endowed with divine gifts that he saw in them special signs of an exceptional affection from heaven for himself, and he counted himself as second to God in his origin as the only son of God. In a word, he avowed that he was, in truth, Christ. But this consciousness of his supermerit, in effect, defined itself in him not as any moral obligation of his towards God and the world, but as his right and prerogative to be before others, and, more than all, before Christ. He had no fundamental enmity towards Jesus. He recognised His Messianic significance and merit, and he really saw in Him his own august predecessor. The moral grandeur and absolute oneness of Christ were not understood by a mind clouded by self-love. He argued thus: "Christ came before me; I appeared next, but that which appears later in time is, in reality, first. I shall come last at the end of history exactly because I am the absolute and final saviour. The first Christ is my forerunner. His mission was to prepare and make ready for my appearance." In this sense the great man of the twenty-first century applied to himself all that was said in the Gospel about the Second Advent, proclaiming that this advent is not a return of the same Christ but a substitution of the previous Christ which is final, that is, he himself.

On this point the coming man does not yet offer much that is characteristic or original. He regards his relation to Christ in the same way as did, for instance, Mahomet, an upright man, whom it is impossible to accuse of any evil design.

The self-loving preference of himself to Christ was justified by this man with such an argument as follows: "Christ, preaching and proclaiming moral welfare, was the reformer of humanity, but I am called to be benefactor of humanity in part reformed, in part unreformed. I shall give to everyone all that is necessary for him. Christ as a moralist divided all people into good and bad; I shall unite them by blessings which are necessary both to the good and the bad. I shall be the real representative of that God who causes the sun to shine upon the good and the bad, and the rain to fall upon the just and unjust. Christ brought a sword; I shall bring peace. He threatened the earth with a dreadful last judgment. But I shall be the final judge, and my judgment will not be a judgment of right only, but of mercy. There will be justice in my judgment; not a justice of reward, but a distributive justice. I shall make a distinction for all, and to each one I shall give what is needful for him."

And behold, in this beautiful frame of mind he awaits some clear, divine call for a new salvation of humanity; for some clear and striking evidence that he is the eldest and beloved firstborn Son of God. He awaits and nourishes his being with the consciousness of his superhuman beneficence and abilities—and this, as it has been said, is a man of irreproachable morality and unusual talent.

The proud and just man waits for the highest sanction in order to begin his salvation of humanity —but he waits in vain. He has passed his thirtieth year and still another three years go by. Suddenly the thought flashes into his mind and pierces to the depths of his brain with a burning shudder, " But if ? if it is not I, but that other—the Galilean. If He is not my forerunner, but the real first and last ? But He must be *alive*—where is He ? . . . If He came to me now and here . . . What shall I say to Him ? I must bend low before Him, as the very simplest Christian, and as a Russian mouzhik murmur stupidly, ' Lord Jesus Christ, have mercy upon me a sinner,' or, like an old Polish woman, prostrate myself before Him, flat on the ground. I, the brilliant genius, the superman!

No, never!" And in the place of the former reasonable and cold respect for God and Christ there is born and grows up in his heart, at first a sort of horror and then a burning envy and fury which seizes and contracts all his being, a hatred which fills his soul. " It is I, and not He. He is not alive and will not be. He has not, He has not risen! He is rotting in the grave, rotting as the lost . . ." With foaming mouth and convulsive bounds he rushed from the house and the garden, and in the heavy, black night ran along the path on the cliffs. His fury had abated and a despair, hard and heavy as the cliff, gloomy as the night, had taken its place. He stopped near a perpendicular break in the cliff and listened to the troubled noise of the water among the stones far below him. An unbearable sorrow crushed his heart. Suddenly there was a movement within him. "Shall I call upon Him—shall I ask Him what to do?" And in the midst of the darkness appeared a gentle and sad image. " He pities me! no, never! He is not risen, He is not risen!" And he flung himself away from the brink. But something as elastic as a waterspout carried him up in the air, and he felt a vibration as from an electric current when some power hurled him back. For an instant he lost consciousness, and when he regained his senses he found himself kneeling a few steps away from the edge of the cliff. Before him was the outline of a figure, bright with a phosphorescent, misty radiance, whose eyes with unbearably sharp brilliancy pierced his soul.

He saw these two piercing eyes and heard,

proceeding neither from within nor from without, a strange voice, dull, as if smothered, and, at the same time, precise and entirely soulless, as if it came from a gramophone. This voice said to him: " My well-beloved son, all my affection is in thee. Why hast thou sought me? Why honour that other, the wicked One and His Father. I am god and thy father. The other—a beggar and crucified One—is a stranger to me and to thee. I have no other son but thee. Thou, my only, only begotten, equal to me. I love thee and ask nothing of thee. Thou art so beautiful, great and powerful. Act in thine own name, not in mine. I do not envy thee; I love thee. I am in need of nothing from thee. He, whom thou didst deem a god, demanded of His Son obedience and boundless subservience, even to the death of the cross, and He was unable to help Him on the cross. I require nothing of thee, and I shall help thee. For thine own sake and the sake of thy special worthiness and superiority and my pure, disinterested love to thee, I shall help thee. Receive my spirit. As, formerly, my spirit brought thee forth in beauty, so now let it beget thee in strength." At these words of the unknown the lips of the superman parted wide, two piercing eyes approached closely to his face, and he felt as if a sharp, icy current was entering into him, filling all his being. Moreover, he felt a marvellous strength, daring, lightness and ecstasy. At the same instant the shining countenance and the two piercing eyes suddenly disappeared, and something lifted the superman from earth and dropped him immediately in his garden near the door of his house.

On the following day not only the visitors of the great man, but even his servants, were amazed at his inspired appearance. But they would have been still more astonished if they had been able to see with what supernatural swiftness and easiness he, having locked himself up in his own study, wrote his remarkable work under the title of " The Open Way to Universal Peace and Prosperity."

The previous books and general activities of the superman had met with severe critics, although they were for the most part especially religious people, and for that reason had no authority of any kind— of course, I am speaking of the time of the coming of Antichrist—so that not many listened to them when they pointed out, in everything that the "coming man" wrote and said, the signs of an absolutely exceptional, intense self-love and conceit, with the absence of true simplicity, rectitude and zeal.

But by his new work he attracted to himself even some of his former critics and opponents. This book, written after the adventure on the cliff, showed in him an unprecedented power of genius. It was something all-embracing and calculated to reconcile all dispute. In it was united a noble reverence for ancient traditions and symbols, with a broad and daring radicalism in social-political demands and requirements ; a boundless freedom of thought with the deepest understanding of all mysticism, unconditional individualism, with a burning zeal for the common good, the most exalted idealism in guiding principles, with the complete definiteness and vitality of practical solutions. And all of it was united and connected with such genius and art that it was easy for every one-sided thinker and worker to see and accept the whole, even from his personal angle of vision, in no way sacrificing truth itself, not magnifying it effectively over his " Ego," not disclaiming the practicability of his one-sidedness nor correcting the faults of his outlook and aims, nor yet completing their shortcomings. This wonderful book was at once translated into all the languages of the civilised—and some of the uncivilised—nations. A thousand newspapers in all parts of the world were filled for a whole year with editorial articles and with the raptures of the critics. Cheap editions, with portraits of the author, were sold in millions of copies, and the whole of the cultured world—which at that period comprised almost the whole earth—was filled with the fame of the incomparable great and only one! No one made any objections to this book— it seemed to each the revelation of entire truth. In it such full justice was done to all the past, all the present was estimated so dispassionately and broadly, and the best future was so clearly and realistically described, that everyone said: " Here is the very thing I need ; this is the ideal which is not Utopian ; this is a project which is not chimerical." And the wonderful author not only attracted everyone, but he was *welcome* to each, thus fulfilling the words of Christ :

" I am come in My Father's name and ye receive Me not ; if another shall come in his own name—him ye will receive." Of course, for the latter to be received he must be welcome.

It is true, some pious people, while warmly praising the book, began to ask why Christ was not once mentioned in it; but other Christians replied, " God be praised! Already, in past centuries, all holy things have been sufficiently soiled by every sort of unacknowledged zealot, and now a deeply religious writer must be very guarded. And if the contents of a book are impregnated with the truly Christian spirit of effective love and universal benevolence, what is there left to wish for?" With this all agreed. Soon after the appearance of " The Open Way," which made its author the most popular of all the people who had lived in the world, the international constitutional assembly of the Union of European States was to meet. This Union, founded after the series of domestic and foreign wars which were connected with the throwing off of the Mongol yoke, and which considerably changed the map of Europe, was faced with the immediate danger of a collision—not between the nations, but between political and social parties. The principal directors of general European policy belonging to the powerful society of Freemasons felt the lack of a common executive authority. European unity, which had been attained with such difficulty, was ready at any moment to fall to pieces. The federated council, or universal committee (*comité permanent universel*), was not in harmony, since not all the places were occupied by real Masons devoted to the matter. Independent members of the committee entered into a separate agreement among themselves, and the matter threatened to cause a new war. Then the "devoted ones" resolved to institute a personal executive authority of one man, with full and sufficient powers. The principal candidate was a member of the Order, "the coming man."

He was the only person with a great world-wide reputation. Being by profession a clever officer of artillery, and by his possessions a large capitalist, he had friendly relations everywhere in financial and military circles. In other and less enlightened times the fact that his origin was obscured by a heavy mist of the unknown would have militated against him. His mother, a person of indulgent conduct, was well known in both hemispheres, but too many different people had good reason to believe themselves his father. These circumstances naturally could not have any significance in a century so much in the van, that even to him it appeared to be the last. The "coming man" was elected almost unanimously as life president of the United States of Europe. When he appeared in the Tribune, in all the glory of his superhuman youthful beauty and power, and in an inspired discourse of great eloquence expounded his universal programme, the assembly, enchanted and carried away, decided, in a burst of enthusiasm and without voting, to pay him the highest honour by electing him as Roman Emperor. The Congress was closed amid the greatest rejoicing, and the great man who had been chosen issued a manifesto which began thus:

"Peoples of the earth, my peace I give to you," and ending with the words, " Peoples of the earth! The promises have been performed. An eternal, universal peace has been secured. Every attempt to destroy it will meet with invincible resistance. For, from henceforth, there is one central authority on earth, which is stronger than all other powers taken separately and together. This invincible, all-subduing authority, with all its power, belongs to me, as chosen autocratic Emperor of Europe. International law has, at last, a sanction hitherto unattained by it. From henceforth no power will dare to say ' War ' when I say it is ' Peace.' Peoples of the earth, peace be to you!" This manifesto produced the desired effect. Everywhere outside Europe, especially in America, strong imperialistic parties were formed which forced their governments, upon various conditions, to join the United States of Europe under the supreme power of the Roman Emperor. There still remained independent tribes and smaller powers somewhere in Asia and Africa. The Emperor, with a small army, but one chosen from Russian, German, Polish, Hungarian and Turkish regiments, accomplished a march from Eastern Asia to Morocco, and without great bloodshed brought into subjection all who were disobedient. He established viceroys in all the countries of both hemispheres, men of European education and native magnates devoted to himself. The population of all pagan countries was dumbfounded, but at the same time enchanted, and proclaimed him a great god. In one year, in a real and accurate sense, he founded a universal monarchy. All tendencies to war were eradicated. The League of Universal Peace met for the last time, and having published an enthusiastic panegyric on the great peace maker, abolished itself as unnecessary. In the second year of his reign the Roman and Universal Emperor issued a new manifesto. " Peoples of the earth, I promised you peace and I have given it you. But peace is beautiful only when coupled with prosperity. He who in time of peace is threatened with the misfortune of poverty, does not find peace a joy. Now, let all who are cold and hungry come to me, so that I may warm them and feed them." Afterwards he announced a simple and all-embracing social reform which, already stated in his book, had there captivated all noble and sober minds. At present, thanks to the concentration in his hands of the world's finance and of a colossal amount of landed property, he was able to realise this reform according to the wishes of the poor, and without sensibly offending the rich. Everyone began to receive in proportion to his ability, and every ability according to its labour and merit.

The new lord of the earth was, before all things, a tender-hearted philanthropist, and not only a philanthropist but a *philosopher*. He himself was a vegetarian. He forbad vivisection, and instituted a strict watch over slaughter-houses. The society for the protection of animals was encouraged by him in every way. But more important than all these details was the solid establishment among all mankind of the most fundamental equality—*an equality of general repletion.* This was accomplished in the second year of his reign. The social-political question was definitely settled. But if repletion be the first interest of hungry people, such people, when once replete, want something more. Even animals, when replete, usually want not only to sleep, but to play. Much more than they, do human beings, who at all times, *post panem*, have demanded *circenses*.

The Emperor-superman understood what was necessary for his people. At this time a great magician from distant Orient came to him in Rome wrapped in a thick cloud of strange happenings and curious tales. It was generally believed among the Neo-Buddhists that he was of divine origin—a son of the sun god Surga and of a water nymph.

This magician, Apollyon by name, was a man undoubtedly talented, half Asiatic, half European, a Catholic bishop *in partibus infidelium*, who, while he was to an astonishing degree in possession of the latest results of Western science and of its technical application, also united with this the knowledge of all that is really sound and significant in the traditional mysticism of the Orient and the skill to make use of it. The results of such a combination were astounding. Apollyon had attained, amongst other things, the skill at once, half scientific, half magical, of attracting and directing atmospheric electricity, and told the people *he brought down fire from heaven*. For the rest, while striking the imagination of the crowd by various unheard-of wonders, he had not up to now made ill use of his power for any personal aims. So this man came to the great Emperor and bowing before him as before a true son of God, declared that in the secret books of the East he had found direct prophecies about him, the Emperor, as the last saviour and universal judge, and placed himself and his art at his service. The Emperor, enchanted with him, received him as a gift from heaven, and after conferring upon him the highest titles, refused henceforth to be parted from him. The peoples of the earth, loaded with the benefits of their lord, were to have, besides general peace and repletion, the possibility, moreover, of constant enjoyment of the most varied and unexpected wonders and phenomena. So ended the third year of the superman's reign.

After the happy solution of the political and social questions, the religious question arose. It was raised by the Emperor himself, particularly in its relation to Christianity. At this time Christianity found itself in the following position. In face of a very considerable diminution in the number of its members there were not more than 45,000,000 Christians left in all the world—morally it had pulled itself up and braced itself and had gained in quality what it had lost in quantity. There were no longer numbered among Christians any people who were not concerned with some Christian spiritual interest. The various confessions of faith diminished proportionately in numbers, and consequently they preserved approximately their former numerical relation. As to their mutual feelings, although enmity had not given place to complete reconciliation, yet it was notably softened and opposition lost its sharpness. The Papacy had already for some time been driven out of Rome, and after many wanderings had found an asylum in Petersburg, on condition that it refrained from propaganda both in that town and in the country. In Russia it became noticeably simpler. While not changing the essentially necessary ·composition of its college and officers, it was obliged to spiritualise the character of its activities and also to reduce to a minimum its magnificent ritual and ceremonial. Many strange and enticing customs, although not formally abolished, went of themselves out of use. In all other countries, especially in North America, the Catholic hierarchy had many representatives, firm in will, of indomitable energy and of independent position, who, more strongly than ever, insisted on the unity of the Catholic Church, and preserved for her her international and cosmopolitan importance. As to Protestantism, at the head of which Germany continued to stand—especially after the reunion of a considerable part of the Anglican Church with Catholicism—it purged itself of its extreme negative tendencies, and the supporters of those tendencies openly descended to religious indifference and unbelief. In the Evangelical churches there remained only sincere believers, at whose head stood persons who combined a wide knowledge with a deep religious consciousness, and who tried with all the more effort to revive in themselves a living image of the ancient and original Christianity. Now that political events had changed the official position of the Church, Russian Orthodoxy, although it had lost many of its former nominal members, yet experienced the joy of union with the best part of the Old Believers, and even with many sects of a definitely religious tendency. This revivified Church, though it did not grow in numbers, did grow in spiritual power, and this power it showed especially in its domestic struggle with the extreme sects which had increased amongst the people and in society, sects which were not lacking in the demoniac and satanic element.

During the first two years of the new reign the Christians, frightened and depressed by the series of revolutions and wars that had gone before, respected the new ruler and his peaceful reforms, some from a well-disposed expectation, others with absolute sympathy and burning enthusiasm. But with the appearance of the great magician in the third year, serious apprehensions and antipathies began to arise amongst many of the Orthodox, Catholics and Evangelicals. The evangelistic and apostolic texts, which spoke of the prince of this world and Antichrist, began to be read with more attention and discussed with animation. From certain indications the Emperor suspected a gathering storm and resolved to clear up the matter quickly. In the beginning of the fourth year of his reign he issued a manifesto to all his faithful Christians, without distinction of creed, inviting them to choose or designate a representative, with full powers for a general council under his presidency. His residence at this time had been changed from Rome to Jerusalem. Palestine was then an autonomous State inhabited and governed principally by Jews. Jerusalem was a free and had been made an imperial city. The Christian holy places had remained inviolate, but upon the spacious platform of Kharam-esh-Sherif, from Berket-Israin and the present barracks on one side to the mosque of El-Ak and "Solomon's Stables" on the other, was erected an enormous edifice including, besides the two ancient small mosques, a spacious "imperial" temple for the union of all cults, and two magnificent imperial palaces with libraries, museums and special apartments for magical experiments and practices. In this half-temple, half-palace, the general council was to be opened on the 14th of September. Since the Evangelical religion had no priesthood in the true sense, the Catholic and Orthodox hierarchy resolved agreeably to the wish of the Emperor, and in order to give a certain homogeneity to the representatives of all forms of Christianity, to allow a certain number of laymen, well known for their piety and devoted to the interests of the Church, to have a part in the council. Once laymen were allowed it was impossible to exclude the lower clergy, both black and white. In this way the number of members of the council exceeded three thousand, and about half a million of Christian pilgrims deluged Jerusalem and Palestine. Among the members of the council there were three who especially stood out. The first was Pope Peter II., by right at the head of the Catholic part of the council. His predecessor had died on the way to the council, and a conclave having been convened at Damascus, Cardinal

Simone Barione was unanimously elected and took the name of Peter. He was of humble origin, came from the Neapolitan district, and had become known as a preacher of the Carmelite Order who rendered great service in the struggle against a Satanist sect which was growing in strength in Petersburg and the surrounding country, and which had led astray not only Orthodox but Catholics. Made Archbishop of Mogilef and then cardinal, he was early marked out for the tiara. He was a man of fifty years of age, of middle height and robust constitution, red-faced, with a hooked nose and thick eyebrows. Impetuous and full of ardour, he spoke fervently with bold gestures, and attracted his auditors more than he persuaded them. The new Pope expressed both distrust and dislike of the universal sovereign; especially was this the case as the late Pope, when leaving for the council, had yielded to the insistence of the Emperor and appointed as a cardinal the imperial chancellor and universal magician, the esoteric Bishop Apollyon, whom Peter considered a doubtful Catholic but undoubted impostor. The actual, though unofficial, leader of the Orthodox was the venerable John, very well known among the Russian people. Although he was officially considered a bishop " in retirement," he did not live in any monastery, but constantly travelled in all directions. There were various legends about him. Some believed that he was Fedor Kouzmich brought back to life, namely, the Emperor Alexander I., who had been born about three centuries before that time. Others went farther and affirmed that he was the Apostle St. John the Divine, who, never having died, now appeared openly in the latter days. He himself said nothing about his origin or youth. He was now very old, but hale and hearty, with yellowish, even greenish white curls and beard, tall, thin in body, with full, rosy cheeks and bright, sparkling eyes, sympathetic both in the expression of his face and in his conversation. He was always dressed in a white cassock and cloak. At the head of the Evangelical members of the council stood the learned German theologian Professor Ernst Pauli. He was a dried-up, little old man of medium height, with an enormous brow, sharp nose and clean-shaven chin. His eyes were distinguished by a certain ferociously kind-hearted look. He constantly rubbed his hands, shook his head, twitched his eyebrows in a strange way and stuck out his lips, while at the same time with flashing eyes he gruffly uttered broken sounds: So! nun! ja! so also! He was dressed solemnly —with a white tie and long pastor's coat, and wore the badges of certain Orders.

The opening of the council was inspiring. Two-thirds of the enormous temple consecrated to the "union of all cults" was furnished with benches and other seats for the members of the council, the remaining third was occupied by a high daïs, on which behind the imperial throne and another, lower down, for the great magician—who was at the same time cardinal and imperial chancellor—there were rows of armchairs for the ministers, courtiers and secretaries of state, and on one side a still further line of armchairs, the use of which was unknown.

In the choir was an orchestra and, on a neighbouring platform, two regiments of the guards were drawn up and a battery for triumphant salvos. The members of the council had already celebrated religious services in their various churches, and the opening of the council was to be entirely secular. When the Emperor entered, accompanied by the great magician and his suite, the orchestra played the " March of United Humanity," which served as the imperial international hymn, and all the members of the council arose, and waving their hats shouted three times, " Vivat ! Hurrah ! Hoch ! " The Emperor, standing by the throne, stretching forth his hand with majestic benevolence, said in a resonant and pleasing voice : " Christians of all cults ! My well-beloved subjects and brethren ! From the beginning of my reign, which the Most High has blessed with such wonderful and noteworthy deeds, not once have I had cause to be displeased with you; you have always fulfilled your duty according to your belief and conscience. This concerns me but little. My sincere love for you, dear brothers, longs for some return. I desire that you, not through any feeling of duty, but through a feeling of zealous love, should recognise me as your true guide in every matter which has been undertaken for the welfare of humanity. But, besides that which I am doing for everyone, I should like to show you special favour. Christians ! what can I do to make you happy ? What shall I give you, not as my subjects, but as fellow-believers, as my brethren ? Christians ! tell me what is dearer to you than aught else in Christianity, so that I may in this matter direct your efforts." He stopped and waited. In the temple a dull echo arose. The members of the council whispered among themselves. Pope Peter, passionately gesticulating, was explaining something to those about him. Professor Pauli shook his head and smacked his lips with exasperation. The venerable John, bending over the Eastern bishops and monks, was quietly suggesting something to them. Having waited several minutes, the Emperor turned to the council and, with the same caressing tone, in which nevertheless there sounded a scarcely perceptible note of irony, said: " Dear Christians, I understand how difficult it is for you to give a direct answer. I desire to aid you in this matter. You, from time immemorial, unhappily have been so divided into various sects and parties that you have not perhaps a common object to which you are all attached. But if you are not able to agree among yourselves, then I hope to bring all parties into agreement, as I shall show to them all the same love and the same readiness to satisfy the *true* aspirations of each. Dear Christians, I know that for many, and not the meanest of you, the thing that is dearer than aught else in Christianity is that *spiritual authority* which it gives to its lawful representatives, not for their own profit, of course, but for the common good, since upon this authority is founded a regular spiritual order and moral discipline indispensable to all. Dear brother Catholics! O, how I understand your point of view, and how I should like to rest my empire on the authority of your spiritual head! In order that you should not think that this is flattery and empty phrases, we solemnly declare that it is agreeable to our autocratic will that the supreme bishop of all Catholics, the Pope of Rome, shall now ascend his throne in Rome with all the former rights and privileges of his position and chair, whensoever granted by our predecessors, beginning with the Emperor Constantine the Great. And from you, brother Catholics, I desire, in return for this, only a true and heartfelt acknowledgment of myself as your sole protector and defender. If there is anyone here who acknowledges me as such in his heart and in his conscience, let him come hither to me." And he pointed to the empty places on the daïs. With joyful shouts of "*Gratias agimus Domine! Salvum fac magnum imperatorem*" almost all the princes of the Catholic Church, the cardinals and bishops, a great part of the believing laymen, and more than half of the monks ascended the daïs, and, after making low bows in the direction of the Emperor, took their places. But below in the middle of the assembly, erect and immovable as a marble statue, sat in his place the Pope, Peter II. All who had surrounded him were on the daïs. But the thinned ranks of monks and laymen which were left below closed around him, forming a tight ring, from whence was heard suppressed whispering: "*Non prævalebunt, non prævalebunt portæ inferni.*"

Glancing in amazement at the motionless Pope, the Emperor again raised his voice: "Dear brethren, I know there are among you those to whom the holy tradition of Christianity, with its old symbols, hymns and prayers, icons and divine ritual is dearer than aught else. What, indeed, can be dearer than this to the devout soul? Know, then, that to-day a decree has been signed by me and large sums allotted for a universal museum of Christian archæology in our glorious imperial city of Constantinople for the purpose of collecting, studying and preserving all the monuments of ecclesiastical antiquity, preferably those of the East; and I further ask you to choose to-morrow from amongst yourselves a committee to consider with me those measures which it is necessary to take for the possible approximation of the traditions and institutions of the holy Orthodox Church to modern conditions, morals and customs. Brothers of the Orthodox faith, you who have my wishes at heart, who feel in your hearts that you can call me your true guide and lord, come up hither." A large part of the hierarchy of the East and North, half of the former Old Believers and more than half of the Orthodox priests, monks and laymen with joyful cries ascended the daïs, glancing proudly at the Catholics who were seated there. But the venerable John did not move and gave a deep sigh. And when the crowd round him were greatly thinned, he left his bench and seated himself nearer to Pope Peter and his circle. After him followed the others who had not gone upon the daïs. Again the Emperor began to speak. "I know there are some of you dear Christians to whom the personal assurance of truth and free investigation of the Scriptures is of all things the dearest in Christianity. I think there is no need to expatiate upon the matter.

Possibly you know that in my early youth I wrote a long treatise on Biblical criticism, which made at the time a certain sensation and was the foundation upon which my reputation was built. Probably, in recognition of this, the university of Tubingen has sent me, at this time, a request to accept from it the honorary diploma of Doctor of Theology. I commanded an answer to be given that I accepted it with pleasure and gratitude. And to-day, in addition to the museum of Christian archæology, I have allotted 1,500,000 marks from the yearly budget for the foundation of a universal institute for the free investigation of the Holy Scriptures from all possible points of view and in all possible directions and for instruction in all allied sciences. If there are any of you to whom my sincere goodwill is pleasing and who are able honestly to acknowledge me as their sovereign leader, I ask them to come hither to the new Doctor of Theology;" and a strange smile passed lightly over the beautiful lips of the great man. More than half of the learned theologians moved, though with a certain hesitation and wavering, towards the daïs. All looked round at Professor Pauli, who remained as if rooted to his seat. The learned theologians who had ascended the daïs were filled with confusion, and suddenly one, waving his hand, leapt straight down past the steps and ran to Professor Pauli and the minority which remained beside him. The latter raised his head, and rising with a somewhat vague movement, went past the empty benches, accompanied by his co-believers who had resisted, and sat down with them near the venerable John and Pope Peter and their circle.

The great majority of the council, among which were included almost all the hierarchy of the East and West, found themselves on the daïs. Below there remained only three groups, who were coming together and pressing about John, Pope Peter and Professor Pauli.

The Emperor turned to them and said in a sad tone: " What more can I do for you? Strange people! What do you want of me? I know not. You yourselves, who are forsaken by the majority of your brethren and leaders and are condemned by popular sentiment, tell me what is dearer to you than aught else in Christianity ? " Then, like a white taper, the venerable John arose and gently answered: " For us the dearest thing of all in Christianity is Christ Himself—He alone, all is from Him, for we know that in Him dwells all the fulness of the Godhead in the flesh. From thee, sire, we are ready to accept every good thing, if only in thy generous hand we recognise the holy hand of Christ. And to thy question : ' What art thou able to do for us ? '—here is our answer : ' Confess now before us, Jesus Christ, the Son of God, Who came in the flesh, Who rose from the dead, and Who will come again. Confess Him, and we with love will receive you as the true forerunner of His glorious coming.'" He was silent and fixed his eyes on the face of the Emperor. Something untoward had happened to the latter. Within him arose a diabolical tempest, such as he had experienced on that fatal night. He completely lost all inner equilibrium, and all his thoughts were concentrated upon preventing himself from being deprived of his external self-possession or from betraying himself inopportunely. He made a superhuman effort not to throw himself with wild howls upon the speaker, and tear him to pieces with his teeth. Suddenly he heard a known but unearthly voice : " Be silent and fear not." He kept silent. Only his face, which was dark and deathlike, became all distorted, and sparks flew from his eyes. Whilst John had been speaking the great magician, wrapped in his immense tri-coloured mantle, which covered the cardinal's crimson, seemed to be manipulating something under it ; his eyes flashed in deep concentration and his lips moved. Through the open windows of the temple an enormous black cloud could be seen coming, and it soon became dark. John did not turn his astonished and frightened eyes from the face of the Emperor, till suddenly he sprang back in horror, and looking round cried out in a stifled voice: " Little children, it is Antichrist." At this moment, simultaneously with a deafening clap of thunder a great flash of lightning enveloped the old man. For an instant all were stunned, and when the dazed Christians came to themselves, the venerable John lay dead.

The Emperor, pale but composed, turned to the council : " You have witnessed the judgment of God. I desired not the death of anyone, but my heavenly Father will avenge His well-beloved Son. The matter is decided. Who will contend against the Most High? Secretaries, write : ' The General Council of All Christians, after fire from heaven destroyed the foolish opponent of divine majesty, unanimously recognise the autocratic Emperor of Rome and of all the World as its supreme guide and lord.'" Suddenly a loud and distinct word is heard throughout the temple : "*Contradicitur!*" Pope Peter II. arose, and with flushed face, trembling with anger, raised his staff in the direction of the Emperor. " Our only Lord is Jesus Christ, Son of the Living God. And thou hast heard who thou art. Away from us ! Cain, fratricide ! Away, instrument of the devil ! By the power of Christ, I, the servant of the servants of God, cast thee out for ever, abominable dog, from the city of God, and deliver thee up to thy father Satan. Anathema! Anathema! Anathema !" While he was speaking the great magician moved uneasily under his mantle, and louder than the last anathema the thunder rumbled, and the last Pope fell lifeless. " Thus by the hand of my Father are all my enemies destroyed," said the Emperor. "*Pereant, pereant,*" cried the trembling princes of the Church. He turned and, leaning upon the shoulder of the great magician, accompanied by all the throng, went out slowly by a door behind the daïs. In the temple there remained the two dead bodies and the narrow circle of Christians, half dead with terror. The only one who was not confused was Professor Pauli. It was as if the general horror had aroused all the forces of his soul. He had changed outwardly, he had an exalted and inspired look. With a resolute step he ascended the daïs, and having taken a seat vacated by one of the secretaries of state, he took a sheet of paper and began to write something on it. Having finished, he got up and read out in a loud voice: "To the glory of our only Saviour, Jesus Christ. The General Council of God's Church, gathered together in Jerusalem, after our blessed brother John, representative of Eastern Christianity, had detected in the great deceiver and enemy of God the true Antichrist predicted in God's word, and after our blessed father, Peter, the representative of Western Christianity, had lawfully and rightfully consigned him to eternal separation from the Church of God; now, before these two witnesses of Christ, who have been killed for the truth, we decide to break off relations with his cursed and abominable assembly, and to go into the wilderness, there to await the imminent coming of our true Lord, Jesus Christ." Animation filled the crowd, and loud cries broke forth: "*Adveniat! adveniat cito. Komm, Herr Jesu, komm!* Come, Lord Jesus!"

Professor Pauli wrote and then read out: "Having adopted this first and last act of the last general council, we sign our names"—and he made a sign of invitation to the assembly. All went up on the platform and signed. At the end, in large Gothic script, was written—"*decorum defunctorum testium locum tenens, Ernst Pauli.*" "Now let us go with our ark of the last covenant," he said, pointing to the two who had died. The bodies were raised on stretchers. Slowly, with Latin chants, and with German and Slavonic hymns, the Christians set forth to the entrance of Kharam-esh-Sherif. Here the procession was stopped by a secretary of state sent by the Emperor and escorted by an officer, with a platoon of guards. The soldiers stopped at the entrance, and the secretary of state read out as follows from an elevated position : " The command of his divine majesty ! For the instruction of Christian people and to protect them against wickedly-disposed persons who are causing disturbances and seducing the people, we have recognised it is for the public good to exhibit publicly the bodies of the two agitators, killed by fire from heaven, in Christian Street (*Kharet-an-Nasara*), at the entrance of the great temple of that religion, named The Holy Sepulchre or The Resurrection, so that all may be persuaded of the reality of their death. Their obstinate adherents, wickedly refusing all our favours and madly closing their eyes to the obvious signs of divinity, have, by being obedient to those who were killed by fire from heaven, put themselves outside our mercy and protection in the face of the heavenly Father. They shall be given full freedom with the single prohibition, on account of the public weal, of not being allowed to live in cities or other inhabited places, so that they may not trouble or seduce innocent and simple-minded people with their evil inventions." When he had finished, eight soldiers at the command of the officer approached the stretchers bearing the bodies.

" What is written is being fulfilled," said Professor Pauli, and the Christians who bore the stretchers handed them over in silence to the soldiers, who withdrew through the north-west gates ; but the Christians, issuing from the north-east gates, hurriedly set out from the city, and, passing the Mount of Olives, went towards Jericho, along a road which previously had been cleared of the mob by *gendarmes* and two cavalry regiments. On the barren hills near Jericho it was decided to wait for a few days. The following morning Christian pilgrims arrived from Jerusalem and related what had taken place in Zion. After the court dinner, all the members of the assembly were invited to the great throne room (near the supposed place of Solomon's throne), and the Emperor, turning to the representatives of the Catholic hierarchy, declared that the welfare of the Church evidently demanded from them a speedy choice of a worthy successor of the Apostle Peter; that, according to the circumstances of the time, the election would have to be summary; that the presence of himself, the Emperor, as leader and representative of the whole Christian world, abundantly made up for any omissions of ritual; and that he, in the name of all Christians, proposed that the Sacred College should elect his well-beloved friend and brother Apollyon, thus making the close bond a lasting one and the union between the Church and the empire indissoluble for their common good. The Sacred College withdrew to a special apartment for the conclave, and returned in half an hour with the new Pope Apollyon. Whilst the balloting was taking place, the Emperor gently, wisely and eloquently persuaded the Orthodox and Evangelical representatives, in view of the great new era of Christian history, to put an end to their divisions, trusting to his word that Apollyon would be able to abolish for ever all the historical abuses of the papal power. Persuaded by this speech, the representatives of Orthodoxy and Protestantism drew up an Act for the union of the Churches, and when Apollyon, accompanied by the cardinals, appeared in the throne room, amidst the joyful cries of the whole assembly, a Greek bishop and an evangelical pastor tendered him their document. *"Accipio et approbo et lætificatur cor meum,"* said Apollyon, signing the paper. " I am as truly Orthodox and Evangelical as I am Catholic," he added, and affectionately exchanged kisses with the Greek and the German. Afterwards he went to the Emperor, who embraced him and held him a long time in his arms. At this time some shining spots began to float about the palace and the temple in all directions ; they grew and changed into bright forms of strange things ; flowers unseen upon earth showered down from above, filling the air with an unknown perfume. From on high resounded ravishing sounds of musical instruments, unheard up to that time, which went straight to the soul and transported the heart, and the angelic voices of an invisible choir sang the praises of the new lord of heaven and earth. Meanwhile a strange subterranean rumbling was heard in the north-west corner of the middle palace under *kubet-el-aruakh— i.e., kupolom dush,* where, according to Mussulman tradition, was the entrance into hell. When the assembly, by invitation of the Emperor, moved in that direction, all clearly heard innumerable high and piercing voices—not childish, not devilish— which were crying out " The time has come, release us, our saviours." But when Apollyon, pressing close against the wall, cried out something three times in an unknown tongue, the voices were silent and the rumbling ceased. Meanwhile an enormous multitude of people from all quarters had surrounded Kharamesh-Sherif. At the approach of night the Emperor, together with the new Pope, went out on the eastern staircase, where his presence aroused a storm of enthusiasm. He bowed affably on all sides, and then Apollyon, from a large basket brought to him by the cardinal deacons, repeatedly took and threw into the air magnificent roman candles, rockets and fountains of fire, which had been set alight by contact with his hand, and which were sometimes pearly phosphorescent, sometimes all the colours of the rainbow. And all of them, when they reached the earth, changed into numberless particoloured leaves with full and unconditional indulgences for all sins, past, present and to come. The popular joy passed all bounds. It is true that certain people affirmed that they saw with their own eyes the indulgences change into most repulsive toads and serpents. Nevertheless, the vast majority was in ecstasies and the popular festival continued for several days, during which time the new wonder-working Pope attained to things so wonderful and improbable that to mention them would be altogether useless. Meanwhile on the deserted heights of Jericho, the Christians gave themselves up to prayer and fasting. On the evening of the fourth day as it became dark, Professor Pauli and ten companions, mounted on asses and taking with them a cart, stole into Jerusalem and through side streets past Kharam-esh-Sherif, came out on Kharet-en-Nasar and approached the entrance to the Church of the Resurrection, where on the pavement lay the bodies of Pope Peter and the venerable John. The street at this hour was empty, everybody had gone to Kharam-esh-Sherif. The soldiers on guard had fallen into a deep sleep. Those who came for the bodies found them entirely untouched by corruption, and not even stiff or heavy. Having raised them upon the stretchers and having covered them with the mantles they had brought, they returned by the same roundabout way to their own people, but scarcely had they lowered the stretchers on the ground than the spirit of life entered into the dead. They moved and attempted to throw off the cloaks in which they were wrapped. All with joyful cries began to assist them, and both having come to life, stood up on their feet, whole and sound. And the venerable John began to speak: "So, little children, we have not parted, and now I say to you, it is time to carry out Christ's last prayer about His followers, that they should be one even as He with the Father is one. So for the sake of this unity of Christ we revere, little children, our well-beloved brother, Peter. May he feed the last of Christ's sheep." And he embraced Peter. Then Professor Pauli went up to him. "*Tu est Petrus*," he said to the Pope, "*jetzt ist es ja gründlich erwiesen und ausser jedem Zweifel gesetzt.*" He seized his hand firmly with his own right hand and gave his left to the venerable John with the words: "*So also, Väterchen, nun sind wir ja Eins in Christo.*" Thus was accomplished the union of the churches in the darkness of the night on a high and lonely place. But the darkness was suddenly lightened by a bright splendour and there appeared a great wonder in heaven : a woman clothed in the sun with the moon under her feet and a crown of twelve stars on her head. The apparition remained for some time in one place and then moved slowly towards the south. Pope Peter raised his staff and cried out : " There is our banner, let us follow it." And he went in the direction of the vision, accompanied by both the old men and the whole company of Christians, to the mountain of of God—to Sinai.

(*Here the reader stopped.*)

LADY.—Why don't you continue ?

MR. Z.—The manuscript doesn't continue. Father Pansophia did not succeed in finishing his tale. When he was already ill he told me what more he wished to write " when I am better." But he did not get well, and the end of the tale was buried with him in the Danilof monastery.

LADY.—But, of course, you remember what he told you, so let us hear it.

MR. Z.—I remember only the principal features. After the spiritual leaders and representatives of Christianity withdrew to the Arabian desert, where crowds of believers jealous for the truth flocked to them from all countries, the new Pope was able, without any obstacle, to pervert by his wonders and prodigies all the superficial Christians who had not been disillusioned by Antichrist, and who remained with him. He declared that, by the power of the keys, he had opened the door between life on earth and life beyond the grave, and in fact, communication between the living and dead, and also between people and demons had been accomplished with the usual manifestations, and new unheard-of scenes of mystical debauchery and demonolatry took place. But scarcely had the Emperor begun to feel himself standing upon a firm religious foundation, and scarcely had he according to the persistent inspiration of his mysterious "father's" voice, declared himself the only true incarnation of supreme and universal Divinity, than a new misfortune fell upon him from an unexpected quarter: the revolt of the Hebrews. This nation, whose numbers at that time had reached thirty millions, was not entirely ignorant of the preparations for and the consolidation of the world-wide successes of the superman. When he moved to Jerusalem, secretly spreading the report in Hebrew circles that his principal problem was to establish the world-wide dominion of Israel, the Hebrews recognised him as the Messiah, and their enthusiastic devotion to him knew no bounds. But suddenly they rose in rebellion, breathing anger and vengeance. This revolution, undoubtedly predicted in the Scriptures and tradition, is set forth by Father Pansophia with, it may be, too much simplicity and realism. The trouble was, that the Hebrews, deeming the Emperor entirely Jewish by race, discovered by chance that he was not even circumcised. That very day Jerusalem, and the following day, all Palestine, was

in revolt. The boundless and fervent devotion to
the Saviour of Israel, to the promised Messiah, was
changed into equally boundless and fervent hatred
of the wily deceiver and brazen impostor. All Israel
rose as one man, and its enemies saw with amazement that the soul of Israel, in its depths, lived not
by calculations and the desires of Mammon, but by
the force of a concentrated feeling—in the expectation of and passion for its eternal Messianic faith.
The Emperor, who had not expected such an outbreak, at once lost his self-possession and issued an
edict condemning to death all insubordinate Jews and
Christians. Many thousands and tens of thousands
who had not succeeded in arming themselves were
slaughtered without mercy. But soon an army of a
million Hebrews occupied Jerusalem, and locked up
Antichrist in Kharam-esh-Sherif. He had at his
disposal only a part of the guards, who were unable
to overcome the masses of the enemy. By the help
of the magic art of his Pope the Emperor succeeded
in passing through the lines of his besiegers, and
quickly appeared again in Syria with an innumerable
army of pagans of different races. The Hebrews
went forth to meet him with small hope of success.
But hardly had the vanguard of both armies come
together, when an earthquake of unprecedented
violence occurred, the crater of an enormous volcano
opened by the Dead Sea, about which lay the
imperial army, and streams of fire flowed together
in one flaming lake and swallowed up the Emperor
himself and his numberless forces, together with Pope
Apollyon, who always accompanied him, and for

whom all his magic was of no avail. Meanwhile, the Hebrews hastened to Jerusalem in fear and trembling, calling for salvation to the God of Israel. When the holy city was already in sight, the heavens were rent by vivid lightning, from the east to the west, and they saw Christ coming towards them in royal apparel, and with the wounds from the nails in His outstretched hands. At the same time, from Sinai to Zion, went the company of Christians, led by Peter, John and Paul, and from various other parts hurried more triumphant multitudes: these consisted of all the Jews and Christians who had been killed by Antichrist. They lived and reigned with Christ for a thousand years. With this Father Pansophia wished to end his narrative, which had for its object, not a universal cataclysm of creation, but the conclusion of our historical process, which consists of the appearance, glorification and destruction of Antichrist.

POLITICIAN.—And do you think that this conclusion is so near?

MR. Z.—Well, there will still be much chatter and fuss on the stage, but the whole drama is written to the end, and neither the actors nor the audience will be permitted to change anything in it.

LADY.—But what is the absolute meaning of this drama? I still do not understand why Antichrist hates God so much, while he himself is essentially good, not evil.

MR. Z.—That's the point, he is not *essentially* so. All the meaning is in that. I take back my previous words that "you cannot explain Antichrist by proverbs alone." He can be explained by a simple proverb, "All is not gold that glitters." You know this glitter of counterfeit good; take it away and no real force remains—none.

GENERAL.—But you notice, too, upon what the curtain falls in this historical drama—upon war—the meeting of two armies. So the end of our conversation has come back to where it was at the beginning. How does this please you, Prince? . . . Good heavens! where's the Prince?

POLITICIAN.—Didn't you see, then? He went out quietly in that pathetic passage where the venerable John presses Antichrist to the wall. I did not wish to interrupt at the time, and afterwards I forgot.

GENERAL.—He has taken to flight, I swear it, and that's for the second time. He mastered himself the first time and came back. But this last was too much for him. Well! Well!